THE GREEK ORTHODOX CHURCH

FAITH, HISTORY, AND PRACTICE

✳✳✳✳✳✳✳✳✳✳✳✳✳✳✳✳✳✳✳✳✳✳✳✳✳✳✳✳✳✳✳✳✳✳✳

DEMETRIOS J. CONSTANTELOS

Foreword by
ARCHBISHOP IAKOVOS

THE SEABURY PRESS   New York

281.9
c

FOREWORD

By the Most Reverend Iakovos
Archbishop of the Greek Orthodox Church
of North and South America

THE *Greek Orthodox Church: Faith, History, and
Practice,* by the Rev. Dr. Demetrios J. Constantelos
is a most valuable addition to the growing list of
studies on Greek and Eastern Orthodoxy. It is accurate and concise, as well as informative and practical.
Though brief in content, it is elucidating and authoritative in its correct interpretation of the spirit,
dogma, traditions, and practices of our venerable
faith, which has had an unbroken existence since its

3

founding by our Lord and Saviour Jesus Christ Himself, and its establishment and perpetuation by His Disciples and the Holy Fathers of the Church.

Written with clarity, trueness of feeling, and devotion, it may be used both as a primer for those previously unacquainted with Orthodoxy, and as an instructive source of information and food for thought by the practitioners of our faith. Furthermore, it encompasses much interpretative material that may be of no little value to theologians, even to those well versed in Orthodoxy, for it is sure in its intent and sound in its appraisals of the basic values for which the One, Holy, Apostolic, Catholic Church has always stood.

I am happy to recommend this excellent study and hope for its wide use, with my blessings and best wishes.

PREFACE

THE PRESENT WORK is neither a theological treatise for trained theologians nor a systematic narration of the history, doctrine, ethics, and worship of the Greek Orthodox Church. It is, rather, an interpretative exposition of the essential teachings and the ethos of the Church intended for the educated layman. In writing it, I have tried to answer hypothetical and real questions raised by Orthodox and non-Orthodox, by college students, and by educated laymen in general.

Acknowledgments are made to His Eminence

7

The Greek Orthodox Church

Archbishop Iakovos for reading the present book and for his kind and generous Foreword, and to my friends and colleagues N. Michael Vaporis and Leonidas Contos, who read the manuscript and offered me the benefit of their criticism.

D. J. C.

CONTENTS

INTRODUCTION

THE ORTHODOX CHURCH proclaims an old faith, in fact the oldest Christian faith. However, this faith is deeply fulfilling and profoundly appropriate for modern man.

Man is not only a body composed of many organs functioning together, but a paradoxical and unique spiritual being as well. It is his spirit, his mind, and his ability to think that distinguish him from animals. The manifestations of man's spiritual and intellectual life constitute what we call civilization. As the human body is the concentration of many organs,

11

civilization is a sum of expressions of man's spiritual life.

Science and philosophy, society and the state, the fine arts and religion are the values which, bound together, make civilization. All these values, applied to our historical life, are essential to progress and, therefore, cannot be understood as functioning separately. But of these religion plays a paramount role in man's life, for man is by nature distinctively religious. To deny religion is to deny one's very nature.

Religion offers a combination of values indispensable for an integrated and thoughtful life. It inspires man with the conviction that the profound essences of our spiritual world are eternal, and this conviction leads in turn to the conclusion that there is no power, natural or otherwise, which could obliterate it. It is religion which transfers our spirit from the realm of the senses and of limitations to the sphere of the supernatural and of holiness, where the good, the beautiful, and the pure reign. Through faith religion grants security and inspires certainty, which no other element of man's nature can provide. Perhaps this helps us to understand why it is almost universally acknowledged that the restudy of religion rightfully belongs in the life of modern man. Religion makes valid claims upon us all.

Introduction

Among the several religions of the world must be included the faith of the Greek Orthodox Catholic Church, which is the oldest of the three major branches of Christianity. There are approximately two hundred million people over the world who profess this religious faith.

"No one after drinking old wine desires new; for he says, 'The old is better.' "

Luke 5:39

1

❋❋❋❋❋❋❋❋❋❋❋❋❋❋❋❋❋❋❋❋❋❋❋❋❋❋❋❋❋❋❋❋❋❋❋❋❋❋❋

THE NAME
OF THE CHURCH

THE GREEK ORTHODOX CHURCH is known also as
Eastern Orthodox. Churches called by national
names, such as Russian Orthodox Greek Catholic,
Serbian Orthodox, Ukrainian Orthodox, Hellenic Orthodox, and Rumanian Orthodox, are branches of the
worldwide Orthodox Church. However, Greek Orthodox Catholic and Apostolic are the most befitting
names for this Church, since they are independent of
the national origin or race of her members. Eastern
Orthodox is a historically appropriate name, which

bears witness to the origin and antiquity of Orthodox Christianity, in contrast to Western Christianity. But for our times "Eastern" is a most inadequate term. The boundaries of the "East" have been removed from Eastern Europe and the Near East to the Far East, China, Korea, Japan. Thus Greek Orthodox is a better designation than any other names.

The attributes "Greek," "Orthodox," "Catholic," and "Apostolic" have important implications. The Church is known as Greek. The Christian faith, following its rejection and persecution in Palestine, became established in the Greek world of the Roman empire. It was propagated through the medium of the Greek language; it was interpreted and clarified by the Fathers of Christianity who were either Greek in origin or Hellenized and who spoke and wrote in Greek. Christian creeds and canons were written and codified in the Greek language by local and ecumenical councils as well. The New Testament books themselves and all the important literature of the Christian religion during the age of the great ecumenical councils (the first eight centuries) were written in Greek. Greek philosophical thought and learning were utilized in defining Christian doctrines.

Following the difficult years of persecution and the trials of Christianity in the pagan Roman empire, it was again the Greek Church, the Greek language, the Greek missionaries that carried the message of Christ in both the East and the West. Orthodox Catholicism is known as Greek in contrast to Western Catholicism which is Latin or Roman. The Latin element emerged as a major factor in the history of Christianity only in the West and as late as the fourth century. It is significant that St. Paul writing to the Church of Rome did not use Latin but Greek. Orthodoxy is Greek in form but divine in content and origin; the spirit is of God, but the body in which it appears to man is Greek. Christianity as a whole owes much to Greek culture, and the Christian Church of the first eight centuries bears all the marks of its close relationship to Greek language, thought, and civilization. The distinguished Russian-American theologian Father Georges Florovsky observes that "Hellenism has placed its eternal character upon the church. It has become an inseparable part of her very being and as such every Christian is, to some extent, a Hellene. Hellenism is not simply a phase in the history of Christianity but a cornerstone in its life. . . . There is no Catholic Christian theology outside of Hellenism." Father Florovsky refers, of course, to Christian antiquity, which developed under the influence of the Greek language, thought, piety, mysticism, and rationale. Christianity and Hellenism go hand in hand.

Not only does the Greek Orthodox Church per se owe much to the Greek civilization, but all Christianity derives its origin from this source as well. Greek culture played a highly significant role in the historical development of the Christian faith.

The late theologian A. Cleveland Coxe, editor of the American edition of the "Ante-Nicene Fathers Series," wrote this about the Greek character of Christianity: "Primitive Christianity was Greek in form and character, Greek from first to last, Greek in all its forms of dogma, worship and polity."

Arthur P. Stanley, a liberal and tolerant professor of ecclesiastical history at Oxford, some one hundred years ago wrote in even more liberal terms worth quoting here: "The Greek Church reminds us of the time when the tongue, not of Rome, but of Greece, was the sacred language of Christendom. It was a striking remark of the Emperor Napoleon, that the introduction of Christianity itself was, in a certain sense the triumph of Greece over Rome; the last and most signal instance of the maxim of Horace, *Graecia capta ferum victorem cepit.* The early Roman church was but a colony of Greek Christians or Grecized Jews. The earliest Fathers of the Western Church wrote in Greek. The early popes were not

Italians, but Greeks. The name of pope is not Latin, but Greek, the common and now despised name of every pastor in the Eastern Church. . . . She is the mother and Rome the daughter. It is her privilege to claim a direct continuity of speech with the earliest times; to boast of reading the whole code of Scripture, Old as well as New, in the language in which it was read and spoken by the Apostles. The humblest peasant who reads his Septuagint or Greek Testament in his own mother-tongue on the hills of Boeotia may proudly feel that he has access to the original oracles of divine truth which pope and cardinal reach by a barbarous and imperfect translation; that he has a key of knowledge which in the West is only to be found in the hands of the learned classes."

Modern theologians agree with Stanley's thesis. The leading Roman Catholic theologian Hugo Rahner adds that "God spoke his revelation into the world of the Greek spirit and the Roman imperium, and the Church guards this truth framed in the Greek speech of her sacred Book. . . ; the Universal Church will continue to speak Greek even if . . . Hellas descended into the abyss of utter oblivion."

Therefore, we cannot accuse those theologians of Greek extraction of nationalism because they emphasize the Greek physiognomy of the Church.

The Greek Orthodox Church

In fact we may direct the accusation against those non-Greek theologians who use national names to describe their Church as Russian, Serbian, Syrian, Bulgarian, or others. However, neither should Orthodox Christians of Greek descent abuse the term for nationalistic purposes. One cannot agree less with Father Florovsky's view that "the task of our time, in the Orthodox world, is to rebuild the Christian-Hellenic culture, not the relics and memories of the past, but out of the perennial spirit of our Church, in which the values of culture were truly 'christened.' Let us be more 'Hellenic' in order that we may be truly Christian." The Greek spirit and culture are permanently wedded to the Christian faith, neither of which can be separated from the other without deforming it. Indeed, as Hugo Rahner says, "the heritage of the Greek spirit only attains immortality when it is secure within the shrine of the Logos whose words are recorded in the tongue of Hellas."

The Church is Orthodox. Thus, it embodies and proclaims the *orthe-doxa*, that is, the right faith in Christ. There is no compromise. What Christ taught and His disciples interpreted is still so taught and so interpreted. Nothing has altered. There is a harmony in all essentials between the present Church and the original Church which secures tranquillity and internal balance, thereby preserving the faith from any extreme. The regulator of this harmony and continuity is the Lord Himself according to His own promise (Matt. 28:20; cf. Mark 16:20). The Holy Spirit is with the Church and guides the Church to all the truth (John 14:26).

The term "Orthodox" is not new. It was used by the early Church to distinguish the true faithful from heretics and followers of false teachings. St. Paul speaks indirectly of it when he asserts that in his own time "some shall depart from the faith, giving heed to seducing spirits, and doctrines of devils" (1 Tim. 4:1). Our Lord warns that there are heretics and false prophets even though they come among us in "sheep's clothing" (Matt. 7:15). The Church is Orthodox then in contrast to heresy and false teaching. The Bible refers to Orthodoxy when it teaches against "false prophets" and "false teachers who privily shall bring damnable heresies . . ." (2 Pet. 2:1; cf. 1 Cor. 11:19; Tit. 3:10; Gal. 5:20).

The Church is Orthodox because she teaches the right doctrine about God, man, and the world. She proclaims what is right for man's earthly and eternal life. But the word "Orthodox" does not simply designate the true teaching about God; it also suggests the true faith, the true life, the true worship of the believer. Thus, *orthe-doxa* implies also *orthe-praxe,* right faith and right life.

The social consciousness of the Church has been great. One may safely say that the whole program of social assistance during the Middle Ages was under the aegis of the Church. And, significantly, this program of the Greek Church did not diminish during the Ottoman captivity. In fact the Church pursued a marvelous program of philanthropic activity: hospitals, old-age homes, orphanages, hospices, reformatory institutions were numerous and well organized as early as the fourth century. That is, the historic Church pursued *orthodoxia* in faith but *orthopraxia* in everyday life as well. (The reader is referred to my book *Byzantine Philanthropy: Its Concept and Application in the Empire* for much more evidence of the social consciousness of the Orthodox Church.)

The Church is Orthodox because she is the original Christian Church. In the twentieth century she remains as the depository and the true preserver of early Christian faith, culture, and life, which were universally accepted and attested to in the early centuries of our era. The present Church evidences an unbroken continuity which, by way of the Ecumenical Councils and the Church Fathers, reaches the Apostolic Church and our Lord Himself. Her Orthodoxy is not a static element which makes her a dormant body of creeds and traditions. It is, rather, a living attribute which receives its inspiration from the Holy Scriptures, the Sacred Tradition, and the Fathers of Christianity; that is, it is the work of the Holy Spirit throughout the history of the Church. Orthodoxy, then, is a continuous reinterpretation and vibrant communication of the revelation of God.

The Church is Catholic in that her message of salvation in Christ is destined for the whole of mankind, for "God . . . desires all men to be saved and to come to the knowledge of the truth" (1 Tim. 2:4) and Christ "gave himself as a ransom for all" (1 Tim. 2:6). The doors of the Church are opened to all, with no discrimination as to race or nationality or sex. "There is neither Jew nor Greek, there is neither slave nor free, there is neither male nor female" (Gal. 3:28). The Church is Catholic because she embraces the totality of truth necessary for man's happiness and salvation. Being the Body of Christ on earth, the Church is what her Head claimed to be, "the way, and the truth" (John 14:6). Christ Himself promised that the Holy Spirit would guide the Church "into all the truth" (John 16:13). Jesus prayed that His Church may be sanctified in the truth (John 17:17). The Church is Catholic because her members inhabit all the world and for her there are no limits of time and space. "Go and teach all nations" was the commandment of the Lord (Matt. 28:19).

The last attribute of the Church is Apostolic. The Church was "built upon the foundation of the apostles . . . Jesus Christ Himself being the cornerstone" (Eph. 2:20). She has remained faithful to the Apostolic faith through the Apostolic succession of her officers and through the Tradition of the Church which has secured her unity with the Ancient Church, a unity in the spirit, in faith, and in truth.

The Orthodox Church is not to be confused with the Greek Catholic Church, which is a branch of the Roman Church. In fact, the Church of Rome refers to its members as Catholics of the Greek or Byzantine rite. The Orthodox on the other hand, who commonly use the name Greek Catholic, use it always with other attributes such as Russian Orthodox Greek Catholic, Carpatho-Russian Orthodox Greek Catholic, etc. Greek Catholic alone refers to the Roman branch of Greek liturgical background, which is known also as "Uniate," i.e., in union with Rome.

There are several major differences between the Orthodox and the Roman, including the following: the primacy and the infallibility of the Roman Pope;

the filioque clause; the teachings on purgatory; the immaculate conception and the bodily ascension of the Theotokos. All these are rejected by the Orthodox. In addition there are other doctrinal, ecclesiastical, and administrative differences between the Orthodox and the Latin Churches. The Greek Church recognizes only a primacy of honor to the Bishop of Rome, to the Bishop of Constantinople, and then to other Church leaders for historical reasons. The institution of the Roman papacy as it evolved in the West after the ninth century was foreign to the early Church; thus it has never been accepted in the East. The development of the Roman primacy was one of the major causes for the schism between the Latin West and the Greek East, and it continues to be a stumbling block for the reunion of Christendom since it has become an element of the doctrinal teaching of the Roman Catholic faith. No doubt the idea of the primacy of the Bishop of Rome is in harmony with the Roman imperial tradition, but it is alien to the teaching of Christ and the early Church. The Roman Catholic Church after Charlemagne transformed the primacy of honor into the primacy of leadership and authority, and the Bishop of Rome made claims for the Pontifex Maximus over all Christendom. These claims brought about the final rupture between the Latin West and the Greek East in the eleventh century. The acts committed by the institution of the papacy for over four hundred years caused the Protestant Reformation in the sixteenth century.

Both the New Testament books and the documents of the late first and early second centuries support the Orthodox teaching that the early Church was governed by a board or a synod of bishops. Christ entrusted His gospel to the Apostles, and the Apostles "appointed their successors . . . to be bishops . . . of those who were to receive the faith," as St. Clement of Rome writes. A work of visions called *The Shepherd of Hermas,* written in the first half of the second century, speaks again about "Those who rule the Church [of Rome] . . . and the presbyters who are set over the Church."

Another Father of the Church, St. Cyprianos, Bishop of Carthage (248-258), points out that "the episcopal office and the organization of the Church have come down to us so that the Church is founded upon the bishops and every act of the Church is controlled by these same officers." He further emphasizes that all the bishops are equal in rank and authority. He adds that ". . . neither does any of us [bishops] set himself up as a bishop of bishops, nor by tyran-

nical terror does any compel his colleague to the
necessity of obedience. . . . Our Lord Jesus Christ
. . . is the only one that has the power . . . of pre-
ferring us [the bishops] as the government of His
Church." Cyprianos' views about the equality of the
bishops in the early Church were shared by other
writers of the first three centuries. Firmilian, Bishop
of Caesarea (*c.* 256) is another witness to this prin-
ciple.

But even in the West each bishop was essentially
independent of higher ecclesiastical authority, and
only after the ninth century is there a strong tend-
ency on the part of the Bishop of Rome to assert himself over the rest of the bishops who because of their
weakness needed protection from some strong political or ecclesiastical leader. Political circumstances
contributed to the Western Church: specifically, uni-
fication under an effective head who could exercise
authority over all the clergy and protect them from
political lords became desirable. The papacy, as such,
appears essentially in the eleventh century, when
it was strengthened especially by the activities of the
Cluny movement which aspired to see the Church
united and purified under a central bishop—the
Pope in Rome.

It should be emphasized that as long as the Roman Catholic Church teaches a supremacy of authority and power of the Bishop of Rome over all Christendom, there is little hope for progress in the ecumenical dialogue for reunion of the Churches. In the matter of the ecumenical dialogue the Orthodox Church would have no hesitation to accept the Bishop of Rome as the *primus inter pares,* the first among equals. But she would yield no other ground on this important subject.

As such the Greek Orthodox Catholic Church is the Church of God on earth; she is not a grand division of Christianity but the pure original Christianity; not a body of believers but the Body of Christ on earth: "the pillar and ground of the truth" (1 Tim. 3:15). The Church today teaches the Word of God, the sacrifice of Jesus, the value of the Holy Spirit, the importance of man and his relation to God, exactly the same message which was taught by the undivided Church for a thousand years. Nothing has been added, nothing has been deleted following the great schism; thus the same Christ yesterday, today, and tomorrow and forever (Heb. 13:8). The Orthodox Christians today belong to Christ as they try to live in Him in humility, in prayer, and in holiness; they proclaim Christ as He was revealed, understood, and taught in the undivided Church.

2

✷✷

THE HISTORICAL
DEVELOPMENT
OF THE CHURCH

IN SPEAKING of the historical development of the
Church, we mean here the genesis and evolution
of the Greek-speaking Church, which is the mother
not only of all Orthodox Churches but of all Christendom as well. The Greek Orthodox Church comprises today five administrative jurisdictions, that is,
the Ecumenical Patriarchate of Constantinople, the
Patriarchates of Alexandria and Jerusalem, and the
Churches of Cyrus and Greece. Altogether the
Church counts a membership of approximately

twelve million people living in Greece proper, the Near East, Africa, North and South America, Western Europe, and Australia.

Alexander the Great, who united the Greeks of the mainland and the Asiatic continent, also diffused Hellenism throughout his vast empire. Thus the Greeks came to comprise the dominant element in countries of the Near East and North Africa, especially in the large and metropolitan cities. There are still many Greeks born and raised in such cities as Constantinople (present-day Istanbul), Alexandria, Jerusalem, and other Near Eastern cities who have never been in Greece proper.

The Greek Orthodox Church of today is the Church which was founded by Jesus Christ Himself, was built up by the Apostles, was strengthened by the martyrs, the saints, and the Fathers, and is maintained and propagated by her believers in the modern world.

The first contact of the Greeks with Christ is related by the author of the Fourth Gospel. St. John writes that some Greeks among those who used to visit Jerusalem at the time of Passover, approached Philip and Andrew, the Apostles, and asked to see Jesus (John 12: 20-24). The Greeks as seekers after truth were eager to listen to something novel, to meet the new master.

Since the dawn of history the Greeks have been inveterate wanderers in their search for the truth that sets man free. They have always been cosmopolitan and eager to attend one teacher after the other. The Odysseus of Homer as well as the Odysseus of Kazantzakis is the restless Greek who, for either knowledge, wealth, or the truth, visits many lands and attends many schools of thought and learning.

An ancient author said: "You Greeks [Athenians] will never rest yourselves, nor will you ever let anyone else rest." In the person of Christ, however, the Greeks discovered their "unknown" God and in Him they found "the way, and the truth, and the life" (John 14:6).

Jesus was aware that the Greeks who came to Him were men with searching minds and troubled spirits. Upon His confrontation with them He exclaimed: "The hour has come that the son of man should be glorified" (John 12:23). Indeed, here we have a few Greeks of small consequence and significance so far as members go, but Christ sees through them the Gentile peoples of all centuries and times who would also seek to see Him. Jesus said the hour had come for the Christian *Ecclesia* to be proclaimed outside the limited boundaries of ancient Israel. No doubt the Greeks played a major role in the preaching of the *kerygma* and the teaching of the *didachē* of Christ. The Greeks had found in the person of Christ the eternal *Logos* and the unknown God of their forebears, while Christ discovered in them sincere followers and dedicated apostles of the new Kingdom. It was from this historic meeting between the "unknown" God and the Greeks themselves that Christianity became an ecumenical religion. Christianity and Hellenism embraced each other in a harmonious living faith and culture, thus fulfilling and enriching each other. The Greek Orthodox Church of today is the organism, the faith, and the culture that was born out of the mating between the incarnate *Logos* and Hellenism.

In the history of the Greek Orthodox Church we can distinguish four stages of development. The Apostolic and ancient period comprises the first three centuries and reaches the age of Constantine the Great. The medieval period includes almost ten centuries, to the fall of Constantinople. The age of captivity starts, roughly, in the fifteenth century and ends around the year 1830. It is followed by the modern period.

The first period, for which much has been written by Orthodox and non-Orthodox alike, was marked by both trials and triumphs, defeats and victories, persecutions and propagation of the faith.

34

Greek cities were the first to be evangelized by the Apostles. St. Paul, though a Jew by birth and religion, was totally Hellenized, and Greek was his native tongue. Tarsus, his native city, was an important center of Greek education. It was St. Paul who developed further the relations between Christ and the Greeks. Paul visited and established Christian congregations in all the important Hellenic centers of both the Asiatic continent and the European mainland. The "unknown God," to whom the Greeks had erected numerous sanctuaries in such cities as Athens, Olympia, Pergamum, and others, was explained further, and the Greeks were satisfied to become His disciples. Their new name, "Christians," almost replaced their ethnic name for many centuries. Their national name, "Hellenes," lost its original meaning and significance and became a rather derogatory identification.

Two reasons contributed to this change. After the edict of Caracalla (212) all the Greeks as well as other nationalities of the Roman empire became Roman citizens. Thus from the third century on the Greeks are referred to as Romans or *Romeoi.* Furthermore, with the attempts of Emperor Julian to revive "Hellenism," Hellenism as an ethnic or national name came to be identified with the ancient religious

35

cults, the pagan gods, and ancient classical tradition in general. Hellenism, Hellene, Hellenismus became synonymous with paganism. The Greeks were simply Christians of the Roman empire. This designation persists to a great degree even today. When the Greeks inquire about someone they do not know, they do not ask whether he or she is a Greek but whether the person in question is a Christian. It was the name "Christian" which united many nationalities under the Ottoman captivity.

The Greeks developed a supranational conscience and preferred to identify themselves solely with Christianity. This became especially manifest during the four hundred years of captivity under the Turks. It is significant to note that although the Patriarchs of Constantinople and many bishops of the Bulgarians, Albanians, Armenians, and Slavs were Greeks (but not exclusively so) during the Ottoman period, they did not attempt to Hellenize their subjects, neither did they exert any effort to force them to abandon their liturgical traditions and culture. Of course, every rule has its exceptions. The fact is that the tradition of the Greek Church has been one of religious toleration rather than nationalism. If this had not been true since the late Byzantine centuries and especially since the four hundred years under the Turks, the Greek Church could have Hellenized all the minorities under her aegis, or at least a great majority of them. The great Greek historian, C. Paparrigopoulos, known for his patriotism, blamed the Church for not exploiting numerous opportunities to Hellenize the various Balkan peoples in a period of four hundred years, something which she could have done without much difficulty.

The term "Greek" as an ethnic name began to appear among the Greeks of the High Middle Ages but still it was not commonly used. However, all nations living outside the medieval Greek world (the Byzantine empire), such as Persians, Russians, the Italic peoples, Franks, and others, considered them to be and called them Greeks.

In any case, to be a Greek is to be an Orthodox Christian. For hundreds of years the Greeks did not mind the absence of a national name, so long as they were identified with Orthodox Christianity. The designations "Greek Orthodox" and "Roman Catholic" were unknown in the early and the medieval Church, and they appropriated their particular meaning after the eleventh century.

Nevertheless, the Hellenism of the Asiatic dispersion as well as the Greeks of the European continent played an unprecedented role in the history of Christianity. Antioch, Tarsos, Ephesos, Smyrna, the islands of Cyprus and Crete, Philippi, Thessalonica, Athens, Corinth, Nicopolis were only a few of the many Greek cities and territories which heard the Christian gospel from the mouth of St. Paul or some other Apostle. All the important churches of the first three centuries were Greek or Greek-speaking. Next to St. Paul other Apostles, such as Andrew, John the Evangelist, Philip, Luke, Mark, Titus, and others, labored for the Christianization of the Greeks. As early as the second century we find flourishing churches not only in cities we have just mentioned but also in lesser towns such as Megara, Sparta, Patras, Larissa, Melos, Tenos, Paros, Thera, Chios, and others.

The Greek cities of Asiatic Hellenism as well as those of the mainland produced during this period great martyrs and profound thinkers. Men such as Polycarpos, Ignatios, Aristides, Athenagoras, Anacletos (Bishop of Rome), Clement of Alexandria, Origen, Gregory the Illuminator of the Armenians, Justin, Melito of Sardis, and others were either Greek or Hellenized, and some were born in the city of Athens or were educated there. The persecutions, on the other hand, against Christianity under the Roman emperors Nero, Domitian, Trajan, Marcus Aurelius,

Galerius, and Diocletian affected the Greek East much more than the Western Roman empire. Dionysios, the Bishop of Athens, Aristios of Dyrrahio, Nicephoros, Cyprianos, Dionysios, Anectos, Paulos, Leonidas, Irene, Demetrios, Catherine, Zeno, Eusebios, Zoticos, Theodoulos are only a few of the thousands of martyrs of such cities as Corinth, Athens, Thessalonica, Gortyn of Crete, Philippi, Kercyra, and of other Greek cities. It was their blood which nourished the Christian seed, as Tertullian has rightly observed. The first period in the history of the Church ended with the edict of toleration under Constantine the Great.

Every student of history knows quite well the tremendous contributions of the Greeks to Christianity during the Middle Ages. This was the period of the great Greek Fathers, of immense missionary enterprises, of Christian thought, poetry, and literature. It was the period of the local and ecumenical councils, which formed and defined the Christian faith that is basic to all Christian denominations today. It was also an era of tremendous social concern of the Church.

The Greek Orthodox today consider the following events as outstanding landmarks of their medieval heritage. From the year 325 to 787 seven ecumenical councils were convened to discuss common problems of the universal Church, i.e., to define the Christian faith, to issue uniform canons, to plan their common destiny. The first Ecumenical Synod (325) dealt with the Holy Trinity, while the second (381), third (431), and fourth (451) discussed the issue concerning the person of Jesus Christ. Their decrees are accepted by most Christians today.

Of course, theologians of the Western Churches remind us often that all major heresies originated in the Greek East. No one can deny this, as well as no one can dispute that all of them were defeated on the same ground, by the intellect, the logic, the mystical intuition, and the biblical scholarship of the Greek Fathers or their Hellenized allies of the near East. In a legalistic and sterile climate, such as was the Western Roman world in the Middle Ages, there was no room for intellectual curiosity, discussion, theological or philosophical speculation. Thus, indeed, very few heresies arose there.

The seventh ecumenical council of 787 was once again a victory of the Greek mentality and understanding. Its decisions were reaffirmed by the council of 843, which proclaimed the legitimate place of icons, symbols, and representation in Christian worship. In other synods, such as those during the episcopacy of Photios, the synodical and democratic administrative system of the Church was proclaimed, which was a reaffirmation of the ancient Apostolic tradition.

During this period several ecclesiastical centers stood out that survive today as centers of Orthodoxy, i.e., Constantinople, Alexandria, Antioch, Jerusalem, and the island of Cyprus; with the exception of Antioch, which is under the jurisdiction of Syrian and Arabic Orthodox Christians, all others maintain strong Greek-speaking Orthodox sees.

It was during this period that great Fathers, theologians, monastics, and missionaries flourished. Basil the Great, Gregory the Theologian, Gregory of Nyssa, John Chrysostomos, Athanasios, Cyril, Eusebios of Caesarea, Maximos the Confessor, Leondios Byzantios, Romanos Melodos, Tarasios, John Eleemon, Photios, Cyril and Methodios, Nicholas Mysticos, Michael Kyrullarios, Cyril Phileotes are but a few of the many churchmen who made Christianity a vital and redeeming force for the Middle Ages.

One cannot overemphasize the outstanding contributions of the Church of Constantinople to propagate the Christian faith to natives of eastern Asia Minor, to the tribes and peoples of central and eastern Europe. The Greek brothers Cyril and Methodios from Thessalonica, the Apostles to the Slavs, were missionaries of culture and civilization as well as of religion.

Highly educated, Cyril and Methodios undertook to form a written alphabet for the Slav nations to translate the Bible and sacred books to their tongue, to shape their worship and adopt new ways of thinking and living. Bulgarians, Pannonians, Moravians, Czechs, Russians, and other tribes "rejoiced to hear the greatness of God extolled in their native tongue" as the Russian Primary Chronicle puts it.

Furthermore the Church manifested a brilliant social consciousness during this period. St. Basil, John Chrysostomos, John Eleemon, Justinian, Theophilos, Constantine IX, John II Comnenos, and many other churchmen and emperors inaugurated tremendous social welfare programs, all of which were under the aegis of the Church. Hospitals, old-age homes, orphanages, reformatory institutions, hospices, leprosaria, and other philanthropic institutions were situated next to churches and monasteries. The monastic communities of such cities or regions as Constantinople, Jerusalem, Alexandria, Attica, Ephesos were great social forces in the work of the Church. The social consciousness and welfare work of the

Greek churches and their monasteries are monuments of praise and worth for all centuries.

The development and cultivation of literature, art, and culture during the Middle Ages is another important chapter in the history of the Greek Church. Greek Church poetry is incomparable and comprises many large volumes in the Church today. Byzantine art is becoming more and more popular these days. It is an achievement in itself. Monasteries were praying communities and working and artistic laboratories as well. The art of calligraphy, together with the transcription of classical and Church Fathers, was highly encouraged by the Church.

In brief, the Greek medieval Church, notwithstanding her shortcomings, was a very positive and constructive institution for the propagation of Christianity and the preservation and propagation of Greek and Roman culture. It was during this period, however, that Latin Christianity, which had been isolated for several centuries, followed its own course to the extent that it broke away from its roots and its unity with Greek Christianity. The great schism of the Roman Church from the Greek Patriarchates was the result of many factors, such as linguistic, cultural, theological, and political.

It was the Western Church which estranged itself from the Eastern Church. Since 330 the capital of the empire was in Constantinople. The city of Constantine became the commanding center of the Greco-Roman world. By abandoning old Rome and moving to the Greek East, Constantine indicated that the future of the empire lay in the East. The Byzantine Greeks almost ignored the developments in the Western Church. Outside of lip service—which they paid to the sole Patriarch of the West as the "first among equals" in honor, as the bishop of the old capital—they never considered the Roman bishop as the Pontifex Maximus. The relations between the two divisions of Christendom were intensified after the ninth century when the Holy Roman empire emerged in the West together with several powerful popes, such as Nicholas I (858-867), who thought of extending their authority to the East, as they had been the commanding ecclesiastical figures in the West. After several confrontations there came an apex in the year 1054, which is traditionally considered the date of the great schism. The major problem in the dispute was the Roman claims of primacy, which would arbitrate in all matters of faith, morals, and administration. The Greek East, which knew of no such precedence, refused to accept the papal claims and

44

made her position clear. The Orthodox position toward the Roman claims can be found in the answer of Nicetas, Archbishop of Nicomedia, to Anselm, Bishop of Havelberg, in the twelfth century. To several accusations of Anselm, Nicetas responded as follows:

"My dearest brother, we do not deny to the Roman Church the primacy amongst the five sister Patriarchates (Rome, Constantinople, Alexandria, Antioch, and Jerusalem), and we recognize her right to the most honourable seat at an Ecumenical Council. But she has separated herself from us by her own deeds, when through pride she assumed a monarchy which does not belong to her office. . . . How shall we accept decrees from her that have been issued without consulting us and even without our knowledge? If the Roman Pontiff, seated on the lofty throne of his glory, wishes to thunder at us and, so to speak, hurl his mandates at us and our churches, not by taking counsel with us but at his own arbitrary pleasure, what kind of brotherhood, or even what kind of parenthood can this be? We should be the slaves, not the sons of such a Church, and the Roman see would not be the pious mother of sons but a hard and imperious mistress of slaves. . . . In such a case what could have been the use of the Scriptures? The writ-

45

ings and the teaching of the Fathers would be useless. The authority of the Roman Pontiff would nullify the value of all because he would be the only bishop, the sole teacher and master."

It is unanimously accepted by historians that the two worlds were further divided as a result of the inhumanity and brutalities that the crusaders inflicted upon the Greek East. The "macabre expression of a pagan death-wish" of the crusaders, in the words of a modern Western historian, brought the final rupture between Roman Catholicism and Greek Orthodoxy. The fall of Constantinople of the crusaders in 1204 marked the beginning of the end of the medieval period of the Greek Church, which now entered into her darkest centuries.

The fall of the Greek Church under the Turks was completed in 1453 when Constantinople, the last great citadel of Greek Orthodoxy in the Middle Ages, fell under the Ottoman Turks. At the beginning, the Church seemed to thrive under the privileges which were granted her by the conqueror Mohammed II. The Patriarch, and actually every bishop in his own diocese, was invested with both religious and political powers—and each one of them became the spokesman of his flock. The Patriarch of Constantinople as well as Metropolitans of great sees came to be known as "ethnarchs," a title that the Archbishop of Cyprus maintains today, i.e., religious and national spokesmen of their peoples. However, the Ecumenical Patriarch, who had been acknowledged as the "first among equals" in the East, became the most important religious leader of all Christians under the Turks. A few of them proved unworthy hierarchs, while others rose above the temptations, the corruption, and the pressures of the sultans and proved worthy representatives and martyrs for the sake of Christ.

Many patriarchs and other clergy of the Orthodox Church who refused to obey the whims of the sultans were either dethroned, exiled, or (as was the case with most of them) put to death. A few illustrations may suffice to substantiate this point. Joachim I (1504) was dethroned; Cyril Loukaris (1638), Cyril Kontaris (1639), Parthenios II (1651), Parthenios III (1657), Gregory V (1821), and others were put to death; Neophytos V (1707) was thrown into the galleys, while several others, such as Jeremias II (1769), Anthimos III (1824), Chrysanthos (1826), and Agathagelos (1830), were sent to exile. Anything but religious toleration was the policy of most of the Ottoman sultans. In addition to heavy taxation upon the Christians, the insolences and arbitrary actions

47

of the Turkish autocracy, the Church suffered from
confiscations of its houses of worship and property
—and Christians were forced to deny their faith and
adopt the Moslem religion.

As a result of many outbreaks of Islamic fanaticism
during those four centuries, the Greek Church manifested also a great deal of vitality. No epoch which
produces martyrs can be described as morbid and
corrupt. In particular during the sixteenth and the
seventeenth centuries many Orthodox witnessed
their faith "unto death." The Greek Church commemorates the names of many neo-martyrs who
preferred death rather than to deny their Christian
faith. Here are a few names of neo-martyrs: Michael Mauroides; Gabriel the Younger; Theodore of
Mytilene; Christodoulos; Cyril of Thessalonica, who
was a young man of twenty-two when he was
burned alive on July 6, 1566; Mark Kyriakopoulos,
who was beheaded in 1643 at Smyrna; John, a young
boy of fourteen, who was put to death in 1652. There
were numerous others.

This information, objective as it is, comes to us not
only through Greek primary sources, but through
the observations of Western travelers or civil servants who served in various cities of the Ottoman empire. For example, the British Consul Paul Ricaut, sta-

tioned in Smyrna, wrote *circa* 1678 that "the increase
and prevalency of the Christian faith against the vi-
olence of kings and emperors, and all the terrours
of death, is a demonstration of its verity; so the stable
perseverance in these our days [i.e., 1678] of the
Greek Church therein, notwithstanding the oppression and contempt put upon it by the *Turk,* and the
allurements and pleasures of this world, is a confirmation no less convincing than the miracles and power
which attended its first beginnings: for indeed it is
admirable to see and consider with what Con-
stancy, Resolution, and Simplicity, ignorant and poor
men keep their Faith; and that the proffer of worldly
preferments, and the priviledge which they enjoy by
becoming *Turks,* the Mode and Fashion of that
Country which they inhabit . . ." would have induced the Greeks to denounce their faith. However,
the Greeks showed much perseverance to their faith.
Ricaut adds that much of their success "is to be attributed herein to the Grace of God, and the promises of the Gospel."

Thus, on the one hand, the Greek Church suffered
from the Turkish and Islamic oppression and persecution, and on the other, the Church suffered from the
propaganda, the intrigues, and the proselytizing activities of the Jesuits, the Cappuchins, the Uniates,

and several Protestant denominations. Paul Ricaut
adds: "But not only hath the *Greek* Church the
Turk for an enemy and an oppressor, but also the
Latines; who not being able by their missionaries to
gain them to their party, and persuade them to re-
nounce the jurisdiction of their Patriarchs, and own
the authority and supremacy of the Roman bishop,
do never omit those occasions which may bring them
under the lash of the Turk, and engage them in a
constant and continual expence; hoping that the people being oppressed and tyred, and in no condition
of having relief under the protection of their own
Governors, may at length be induced to embrace a
foreign Head, who hath riches and power to defend
them. Moreover, besides these wiles, the Roman
Priests frequent all places, where the Greeks inhabit, endeavouring to draw them unto their side
both by preaching and writings. . . ." Therefore the
late British scholar A. H. Hore of Trinity College,
Oxford, rightly observed: "The fall of the Eastern
Empire and the low state to which the persecuted
Greek Church fell, and from which it is little less than
a miracle that it should now be recovering, is a chapter of dishonour and disgrace in the history of Western Europe."

No doubt, the Greek Church found herself be-

tween various adversaries whose only objective was
to convert her faithful to their own creeds. However, much decay originated from within the administration of the Church. Simony, quarrels, pov-
erty among the clergy contributed to the already low
state of the Church. Indeed one cannot agree less
with the view of modern historians who write that
"the survival of the Greek Church under four centuries of Turkish rule is no less than a miracle."

The modern period in the history of the Greek
Church begins with the liberation of a considerable
segment of Hellenism from the Turks in the 1830's.
In addition to five self-governing, Greek-speaking,
autocephalous Orthodox Churces, namely the Ecumenical Patriarchate of Constantinople, the Patriarchates of Alexandria, Antioch, and Jerusalem, and
the Church of Cyprus, the autocephalous Church of
Greece was added.

Looking at the present state of the Greek-speaking
Orthodox Jurisdictions, the Ecumenical Patriarchate,
with jurisdiction over the Greek Orthodox of Western Europe, North and South America, Australia,
and several islands of Greece, has a membership of
approximately two and one-half million. The Ecumenical Patriarch, who heads it, is respected by all
Orthodox as the chief among equals and serves as

the strongest link of unity among all Orthodox.
Despite the harassments which have been placed
upon its life and activities by the Turkish govern-
ments in the past decade or so, the Patriarchate
stands as the most important citadel in all Orthodoxy. It maintains an excellent theological school,
and its initiative and contributions to the ecumenical
movement is an outstanding example of a progres-
sive, suffering church.

Among the outstanding contributions of the Ecumenical Patriarchate in recent years we may count
several. Many endeavors have been undertaken in
order to bring into closer cooperation all the autocephalous Orthodox Churches of the world. The Patriarchate aspires to accomplish a federation of all
Orthodox Churches and to make their spiritual unity
visible in their administrative cooperation as well.
The recent three pan-Orthodox Synods on the island
of Rhodes manifest the spirit of cooperation and the
brotherly love which characterizes worldwide Orthodoxy today.

It was through the untiring efforts of Patriarch
Athenagoras that several Orthodox Churches joined
the World Council of Churches in the last decade.
Furthermore, the Ecumenical Patriarchate has initiated dialogues between the Orthodox, on the

one hand, and the Anglican, the Old Catholic, and the Oriental Churches, on the other. The meeting of Patriarch Athenagoras and the Roman Pope Paul VI eased the way, and a new era was inaugurated in the relations between the Greek Orthodox and the Roman Catholic Churches. This was achieved through the personal efforts of the Ecumenical Patriarch, who has proved himself an apostle of love, understanding, and cooperation toward all Christians.

Despite its limited resources, the Ecumenical Patriarchate is very active in social and philanthropic projects. It maintains forty philanthropic societies which administer to the needs of the poor in Istanbul and elsewhere. These societies are under the supervision of the *Pneumatike Diaconia,* or Spiritual Diaconate. Children are of special concern to this patriarchal organization. It helps poor boys and girls from their early years and sees them through college. *Pneumatike Diaconia* grants several scholarships every year and often helps students even during their graduate studies abroad. In addition to many scholarships, the Patriarchate supports summer camps for both sexes between the ages of seven and fourteen. More than five hundred students benefit from this program annually. There are camps also for working youth, the benefits of which are extended to more than two hundred annually. These are generous numbers when we consider the fact that the faithful of Istanbul are approximately fifty thousand people.

The Patriarchate spends almost four thousand dollars (thirty thousand Turkish lire) every month for several poor families in Constantinople and provides many thousands of Turkish lire for dowries of poor girls. By the way, the marriage of a poor girl who is under the protection of the Patriarchate takes place in the cathedral of the Patriarchate with a bishop officiating. This practice indicates that the mother Church makes no distinctions and a poor girl is supported as lovingly as any rich and socially prominent.

As one studies the social consciousness of the Ecumenical Patriarchate today, one immediately thinks of the tremendous philanthropic programs of the same Patriarchate during the Middle Ages, that is, the Byzantine era. The Ecumenical Patriarch Athenagoras I, who was elevated to the Patriarchal throne while he was Archbishop of North and South America, has added new dimensions to the Patriarchate and is a man admired for his vision and prophetic charisma.

The Patriarch of Alexandria is the heir of a rich tradition in theological scholarship and missionary activity. It maintains jurisdiction over all Greek Orthodox of Egypt and Africa with a membership of approximately two hundred thousand. Of course, the Church of Alexandria is but a shadow when we compare it with its past. Nonetheless, in view of its most successful missions in several new African nations, such as Uganda and Tanzania, we cannot underestimate its vitality.

The ancient Patriarchate of Jerusalem with a membership of perhaps fifty thousand people, is an important deposition of early Christian tradition and faith. It is known as the guardian of the historic sites of the Holy Land where Jesus was born and taught.

The nearby Church of Cyprus is one of the oldest autocephalous Christian communities. She became self-governing during the sixth century when Justinian granted her special privileges. The Church has suffered much since the seventh century up to recent years as a result of the strategic position of the island and the several masters who have conquered the island. Nevertheless, the Church has survived and counts more than a half million people in membership. It is a vigorous Church with a seminary, three metropolitan episcopates, philanthropic institutions, and periodicals.

The Church of Greece, with a membership of approximately eight and one-half million people, was recognized officially as a self-governed Church in 1850. The Church of Greece increased territorially and numerically in proportion to the enlargement of modern Greece after a series of revolutionary wars which brought to the Greek nation the territories of Epirus, Thessaly, Macedonia, Thrace, the Ionian, and the Aegean Islands. Greece is solidly an Orthodox Christian country, and the Church plays a very important role in the life of the nation. The Church is indeed "the soul of Greece," as an American author observed recently.

The Church is divided into sixty-six small dioceses with approximately 7,765 parishes. Here I wish to emphasize three elements of the vitality and the dynamism of the postwar Greek Church: namely, religious education, social consciousness, and theological scholarship. The catechetical, or Sunday, schools are a source of pride in Greece for clergymen and laymen alike. The religious revivals which were initiated by such movements as "ZOE" (brotherhood of theologians), "Orthodox Christian Unions," "*Apos-*

toliki Diaconia," to mention only the most important of several religious organizations, saved the nation from communism. During the war and postwar years, between 1940 and 1947, the youth of Greece was called to join either communist youth organizations or religious youth societies. Young men and women, perplexed and confused as a result of the brutalities and barbarisms, the injustices and the decay which were introduced by the "civilized barbarians" of the twentieth century, were looking for light and orientation, for promises and fulfillment.

I have known several young men who undoubtedly would have joined the communist movement had they not found a vigorous Church and vital religious organizations, which attracted them away from communism. Often a young man had a choice either to join the EPON (Communist Youth Organization) or the ZOE movement, or some other religious group. The ZOE movement in particular expressed its work through various channels and organizations and reached every class of people. The simple folk as well as the university professor, the young laborer and the university student, the parent as well as the young girl could find in the Church, through ZOE or some other organization, a place of hope, love, and care. The catechetical schools reached their zenith of success and activity. Until 1954 the Church of Greece counted more than 7,750 Sunday schools. "Sotir" (brotherhood of theologians) is another new but very important movement of recent years.

As a result of the postwar revivals Church attendance increased greatly, Bible study became common, participation in the sacraments of sacred Confession and Holy Communion frequent, and the social consciousness of the Church flourished to an unprecedented degree.

Unfortunately very little is known about the social consciousness of the Greek Orthodox Church by non-Orthodox. This aspect requires perhaps a longer treatment than the following few remarks. A non-Orthodox colleague told me recently: "My fellow colleagues at the theological school of our university do not think highly of your Church because of her lack in social concern." While I was waiting for the commencement exercises of the local high school in Lexington, Mass., a Protestant minister was greatly surprised when I told him of the concern and the involvement of the Greek Church for the improvement of the social order.

Every diocese of Greece is a center of philanthropic activity. Not only has the Church issued encyclicals expressive of her concern for social justice, but each bishop has a treasury of "Funds for the Poor," and maintains several welfare institutions. There are more than 140 orphanages, old-age homes, nurseries, sanatoriums, clinics, hospitals, schools for retarded children, and other philanthropic establishments, which are maintained directly by the dioceses. For example, the diocese of Dimitrias with 124 parishes maintains twelve charitable institutions. The diocese of Messenia with a population of perhaps 100,000 supports fourteen philanthropic establishments. The diocese of Lesbos with sixty parishes supports twelve welfare institutions.

The welfare concern of the Church is often extended to include dowries for poor orphan girls, distribution of funds to individuals released from prison, distribution of foodstuffs, clothing, and footwear to poor families, schoolchildren, and individuals in want. Many dioceses support needy students of theology or students of other disciplines and of graduate departments.

Every parish also has a relief treasury, or *logia,* for the needs of the local poor people or traveling needy individuals. But the social consciousness of the Greek Church is best expressed when disasters strike, such as in the war years and the subsequent foreign occupations, the disastrous earthquakes of the Ionian Islands and Thessaly, and other catastrophes. It is not an exaggeration to say that the Church has often proved to be a bastion of social justice and the vanguard of welfare and relief programs.

It is not irrelevant to state here that during the German occupation of Greece in the 1940's the Church of Greece intervened numerous times to save the Jewish people of Greece. The late Archbishop Damaskinos offered special housing and all the necessary means in order to save the Greek Jewry. He made himself and the Greek Church responsible for their future. Damaskinos' endeavors failed, but the good will and the humanism of the Greek Church became manifest.

The social work of the Greek Church was extended to protect and save British and Australian soldiers who were left behind after the German occupation of Greece. There is no other Church which suffered so much from the Axis occupation of Greece and the communists alike during the decade of 1940-1950. More than four hundred clergymen were killed either because they were men of religious principles or because of patriotism. A substantial sacrifice indeed from a Church with no more than seven thousand clergymen.

All in all, the Greek Orthodox Church, considering

the limitations placed upon her by political upheavals and historical circumstances as well as the means at her disposal, is conscious of her heritage and maintains, even though in a lesser degree, the tremendous social consciousness of the medieval and ancient Church.

The third aspect which requires our special attention is the vitality of theological scholarship in the Greek schools of theology today. It is not an exaggeration to state that during the last fifty years Greece has produced great theologians of international status. In addition to two schools of theology, the Church supports several seminaries for the training of parish priests. The concern of many theologians is both academic and ecclesiastical.

It is not true that Greek theology is only "a theology of the university lecture room." The contributions of such theologians and scholars as P. N. Trembelas, P. Bratsiotis, J. Panagiotides, J. Karmiris, J. Cotsonis, A. Theodorou, and E. Theodorou are both academic and kerygmatic. Prof. Dr. Trembelas in particular, Rev. Prof. Dr. Cotsonis, Prof. Dr. E. Theodorou, Dr. C. Kourkoulas, Dr. B. Moustakis, and several others have produced works for the academician and the theologian as well as for the ordinary layman. They are men of university rank and of the pulpit. There were several theologians in the 1920's and 1930's, and there are several others today, whose "intrinsic worth . . . is such that any company of modern scholars would gladly and gratefully admit them to their fellowship," as the late theologian Frank Gavin once said.

Greek Orthodox theology has served often and will continue to serve as a *martyria*, a witness to the theology of the early and the medieval Church; it has contributed significantly to the ecumenical movement through such churchmen as Germanos, the late Archbishop of Thyateira, the late Archbishop Michael, Archbishop Iakovos, Professor Hamilcar Alivizatos, and Professor Nikos Nissiotis. Under the aegis of the Ecumenical Patriarchate, Greek Orthodox theology will continue to work for the restoration of the Christian world *and the unity of the Church.*

The Greek Orthodox Church of Constantinople, Alexandria, Jerusalem, Cyprus, and Greece, together with churches of other Orthodox Jurisdictions comprise the Church which was born as a result of the meeting between Jesus Christ, the eternal *Logos* and the Greeks in the city of Jerusalem some 1,930 years ago.

3

****

THE FAITH
OF THE CHURCH

WHAT EXACTLY does an Orthodox Christian believe? Is his faith identical with or similar to
the Protestant or the Roman Catholic faith? Or is it
unique? The Greek Orthodox Christian is neither a
Roman Catholic nor a Protestant. His beliefs might
be considered to be unique in the sense that he is a
living member of and in organic unity with the original Church. In every Sunday or weekday Liturgy the
Orthodox Christian proclaims:

"I believe in one God, Father Almighty, Maker of

Heaven and Earth and of everything visible and invisible. And in one Lord Jesus Christ, the only begotten Son of God, begotten of the Father before all ages. Light of Light, True God of True God, begotten not made, consubstantial with the Father, through Whom all things were made. Who for us men and for our salvation came down from Heaven, and was incarnated by the Holy Spirit and of the Virgin Mary, and became Man. Crucified for our salvation under Pontius Pilate. He suffered and was buried. And was resurrected on the third day according to the scriptures. And ascended into Heaven, and sits at the right hand of the Father; and He will return in glory to judge the living and the dead; Whose reign will have no end. And I believe in the Holy Spirit, the Lord, the Giver of Life. Who proceeds from the Father, Who together with the Father and the Son, is worshipped and glorified; Who spoke through the Prophets. I believe in One, Holy, Catholic and Apostolic Church. I acknowledge one baptism for the remission of sins. I await the resurrection of the dead, and the life of the Ages to come."

This is the faith of the Orthodox Church in its briefest form. It was the faith of undivided Christendom before the eleventh century, formulated by the unanimous deliberation of the representatives of all Christendom in the two great ecumenical councils, of

Nicaea (325) and of Constantinople (381). It is known as the symbol of faith or the creed.

The essence of the faith can be rendered in a sentence: The Orthodox faith presents God revealed in Jesus Christ and man redeemed by Jesus Christ. God appeared among men in time and space to redeem man and reconcile him with Himself. "God was made man that man may become God," as St. Athanasios asserted. The Son of God Jesus Christ became manifest among men in order to regenerate man and make him a new creation through the Holy Spirit, "the Giver of Life."

Man becomes a new creature within the Church, because she is the depository of grace and the means of salvation. The Orthodox Church is not a worldly organization or a social system, but a living organism with Christ as her head. Her members are animated by the common means of sanctification: the sacraments, the reading of the Word of God, and the life of prayer. The Orthodox Church is rightly known as the Church of prayer and profound spirituality. The faithful believe in Christ, live through Christ, worship with Christ. Their faith in Christ is sustained and guarded by the Church as a whole, the conscience of the Church, which is the totality of the faithful, laymen and clergymen alike.

The Orthodox Christian strives to live in Christ.

Love and charity, justice and humility, these have been emphasized in all Greek Orthodox societies. Their ethics are Christ-centered ethics. This fact explains why there are fewer delinquents, criminals, and broken homes here than in many other religious societies. In fact, Greek Orthodox ethics may be considered strict for the present age. But they bear good fruit worthy of any sacrifice. The Greek Orthodox Catholic Church in America is indeed proud of its record in this respect.

The Orthodox Church has "Mysteries," which correspond to what Western Christianity describes as "sacraments." There are a number of mysteries in Christianity; for example the mysteries of faith, the doctrine of the Holy Trinity, the belief in two perfect natures of Christ, the procession of the Holy Spirit, Redemption, and the like. But by "Mysteries" we mean here specific means of grace given by God directly or indirectly to His Church through the Holy Spirit Who penetrates into every aspect of man's life.

Through these Mysteries, or sacraments, the regenerating, justifying, and sanctifying Grace of God is bestowed upon the faithful. And though these Mysteries transmit supernatural grace, they convey it to man by external and visible means and acts. That is, the Mysteries of the Church, like the Church herself, include both supernatural and material elements. The theanthropic, the divine, and the human nature of Christ is extended to both His Church and to her means of grace as well.

4

❖❖

THE MYSTERIES
OF THE CHURCH

T HE CHURCH has not accepted any number of
Mysteries by a formal decree. However the
following have been accepted as Mysteries *de facto*.
Baptism: It is through this sacrament that one enters
the threshold of the earthly Kingdom of God, and
becomes a member of the Church. Through Baptism
one receives forgiveness of sins and becomes a member of the Body of Christ. "Be baptized . . . for the
forgiveness of your sins" is the command of the Holy
Spirit (Acts 2:28; cf. Acts 22:16). Baptism, of course,

presupposes faith in Christ and a determination to live the Christian way of life. Ever since the practice of infant Baptism was introduced in the early Church, the creed of faith is pronounced by the child's sponsor. Together with the parents, the sponsor sees that the child is brought up in the Christian Orthodox faith.

Most Orthodox Christians today are born in the Orthodox faith. But there are many who are converted from other religious or Christian creeds. An example of this may be the group conversions of Moslems to the Orthodox faith in northern Greece in recent years. While the Church does not preach the gospel among people where Christ is accepted, there are every year numerous converts from various Christian bodies in such countries as Great Britain, France, Germany, and the United States of America. These converts choose the Orthodox faith freely and willingly.

Outside the United States, the Greek Orthodox Church has missions in Tanzania, Mexico, Uganda, Korea. Today there is an ever increasing zeal for missionary activity in non-Christian territories. Unlike some denominations that make every effort to convert other Christians to their creeds, the Greek Church follows St. Paul, who said: "I strived to preach the gospel, not where Christ was named, lest I should build upon another man's foundation: but as it is written, to whom he was not spoken of, they shall see: and they that have not heard shall understand" (Rom. 15:20-21).

It is indeed unfortunate that there are Christian groups which send missionaries to such Christian countries as Greece. Professor Edward Jurji, of Princeton Theological Seminary, speaking of some missions in the Middle East, admitted that they are successful in converting only a few Christians to their denominations while they fail to convert non-Christians.

Our friends of such misinformed groups must take heed lest the words of Christ apply to them: "Woe unto you . . . for ye compass sea and land to make one proselyte, and when he is made, ye make him twofold more the child of hell than yourselves" (Matt. 23:15).

In the domain of religious education, the Greek Orthodox Church conducts catechetical classes, a program which corresponds to Sunday schools. Practically every Greek Orthodox parish today in the United States, in addition to cathechetical classes, holds religious lectures and Bible classes regularly. The system of catechetical classes is well organized, especially in Greece under the auspices of the *Apos-*

toliki Diaconia and the ZOE brotherhood of theologians.

Following Baptism comes the sacrament of Holy Chrismation. It is administered immediately after Baptism and corresponds to the "laying on of hands" or "chrism with oil" of the New Testament times. Through this sacrament the newly baptized receives the seal and the gifts of the Holy Spirit (Acts 2:38); it constitutes the completion of Baptism. It could be compared to Confirmation, which is practiced in non-Orthodox churches.

In addition, the faithful need constant spiritual nourishment, food for the preservation and cultivation of their spiritual life. Thus there is the sacrament of the Holy Eucharist. "He who eats my flesh and drinks my blood abides in me and I in him" (John 6:56; cf. Matt. 26:26). Since the Orthodox believe in the real presence of Jesus in the sacrament, Holy Eucharist occupies a very important place in the life of the Orthodox Christian. The answer to the question why the Orthodox Catholic Church places such an emphasis on the Eucharist must be sought once again in the Holy Scriptures.

As is well known, the mental attitude of the Jews and the Greeks toward religion in the New Testament times is described characteristically by St. Paul.

"The Jews ask for signs and the Greeks search for wisdom" St. Paul writes to the Corinthians (1 Cor. 1:22).

The Jews, as chosen people of the Most High, had received innumerable "signs" from God. God proved His faithfulness, His love, and His providence toward ancient Israel by various signs in the Old Testament times. God planned and executed their liberation from Egypt. God gave them manna to eat and water to drink in the wilderness.

Now, in the New Testament times, the Jews demanded similar signs from Christ in order to believe and follow Him. "What sign are you going to perform that we may see it and believe in you?" they ask. Our fathers ate "the manna in the wilderness. . . . He gave them bread from heaven to eat" (John 6:30).

Jesus offers Himself, His very body and His very blood, as the heavenly manna for the nourishment not only of ancient Israel but of the new one as well. Christ explains that the bread which ancient Israel had received was not eternal, it was not from heaven; it was something temporary, material, and perishing. But now He offers "the bread of God which comes from heaven and gives eternal life to the world" (John 6:51-52). This bread of God is Jesus Himself.

"I am the bread of life. He who comes to me will

never hunger, and he who believes in me will never thirst any more. . . . I am the bread of life. Your fathers ate the manna in the wilderness, and they died. This is the bread which comes down from heaven, that a man may eat of it and not die. I am the living bread which came down from heaven; if any one eats of this bread, he will live forever; and the bread which I shall give for the life of the world is my flesh. . . . Truly, truly, I say unto you, unless you eat the flesh of the son of man and drink his blood, you have no life in you; . . . my flesh is food indeed, and my blood is drink indeed. . . . He who eats my flesh and drinks my blood abides in me, and I in him" (John 6:48-56).

Jesus spoke these enigmatic words almost a year before His death. And a few days before His crucifixion, at the Last Supper, Jesus took a loaf of bread and blessed it. He broke it into pieces and gave it to his disciples, saying, "Take this and eat it. It is my body!" And He took the wine cup and gave thanks and gave it to them, saying, "You must drink from it, for this is my blood which ratifies the agreement, and is to be poured out for many people, for the forgiveness of their sins" (Matt. 26:26-28).

By virtue of this evidence the Holy Eucharist is the center not only of our Christian worship but also of

our very lives as well. The Holy Eucharist of the
Greek Orthodox Church is nothing less than the re-
enactment of the life, the teaching, the death, and the
resurrection of our Lord. It is a mystery by which we
commemorate and remember His sacrifice for us; the
offering of His life is the imperishable manna. St.
Paul, writing to the Corinthians, states that he received from Christ the revelation of the significance of
His Last Supper. What he repeatedly indicates is that
Christians must perform this Act of Commemoration
in remembrance of Jesus' sacrifice, of the Lord's
death (1 Cor. 11:23-29).

The term "Eucharist" implies "thanksgiving."
Jesus offered Himself as the supreme sacrifice to God
the Father and commanded this to be done in remembrance of Himself. Thus, the Orthodox priest truly
acts in Christ's stead when he performs the Divine
Liturgy. "He reproduces what Christ did, and he
then offers a true and complete sacrifice to God the
Father" (St. Cyprianos).

We offer the Divine Eucharist as eucharistic worship because man is forgetful. As the observance of
the Passover reminded ancient Israel of its liberation
from Egypt, so it is with the Eucharist, which reminds
us of the sacrifice of the Son of God. This is in perfect
accord with man's nature. We write biographies, we
erect monuments of art, we paint pictures, and we

record histories lest we forget. Thus with the Eucharist. The Divine Eucharist is celebrated as true sacrifice, as remembrance, as communion, and as eucharist.

There is abundant evidence that the Apostolic Church extensively practiced the Eucharist. St. Ignatios of Antioch advises the Christians of Ephesus "to meet frequently to celebrate God's Eucharist and to offer praise" (Epistle to Ephesians, 13). It "is the medicine of immortality, the antidote of death, and everlasting life in Jesus Christ" (*ibid.*, 20).

The Eucharist, therefore, is the new sign which God established between Himself and the new Israel. The faithful—the Christians—must practice the Eucharist as often as possible. It is a sound way to express our thanks to God the Father for the great sacrifice of His Son. This mystery of the body and the blood of Christ is a realization of the unity of all true believers both with Christ and, at the same time, with all the members of His Holy Body—the Church. Through the sacrament of the Eucharist not only are our thanks given to God, but also our nature enters into union with the divine nature of Christ. Our humanity becomes consubstantial with the deified humanity of Christ. Thereby through Holy Communion a corporeal unity of man with Christ is achieved.

5

****

THE WORSHIP
OF THE CHURCH

IT IS THE UNANIMOUS opinion of the early Church that
the Eucharist is spiritual food and drink, not
simply manna and water of the wilderness, but the
very body and the blood of Christ. And this is the new
"sign" which dramatizes the close relationship between God and man. Not a sign similar to those signs
for which the Jews were asking of Jesus, nor a sign
which would be foolishness to the Greeks, but a
"sign" full of mystery and wisdom as well.

This mystery is approached by faith. It may be a

76

perplexing mystery for some people, who insist on miracles, or an illogical absurdity to others, who demand reason, but for us Christians it is God's power and God's wisdom (cf. 1 Cor. 1:24).

The Mystery of the Holy Eucharist is intimately connected with the Divine Liturgy, which is the chief act of Greek Orthodox public worship. In fact these two terms are used interchangeably. Divine Liturgy is used often as a title of the Holy Eucharist, while the latter implies the Divine Liturgy.

In speaking of the Divine Liturgy here we signify a public service of approximately two hours that is a worshiping testimony of the Revelation of God. It unfolds before the worshipers the essence of the theology, the mystical existential character, and the devotional traditions of Greek Orthodoxy.

The Liturgy is a gradational or step-by-step depiction of God's revelation as it happened in both the Old and the New Testament periods. Through symbolic utterances, gestures, signs, and symbols, the whole redemptive plan of God is set before the congregation. The central theme however is the life of Christ, from His birth in Bethlehem to His ascension, which is unrolled in unparalleled beauty, profundity, and movement.

According to the Russian Primary Chronicle, it was

because of the wonder and impression that the Liturgy left upon a Russian delegation to Constantinople that the Russians adopted Greek Orthodoxy. When Vladimir, Prince of Kiev, decided to investigate in order to determine which religion was appropriate for his young nation, in the tenth century, he sent emissaries to Constantinople, the capital of the Greek medieval world. The delegates attended the Divine Liturgy in the magnificent Church of Hagia Sophia in order "to examine the Greek faith" as the Russian source puts it. The Russian delegates reported to their prince, his boyars, and his elders, that when they attended the Divine Liturgy they did not know whether they were in heaven or on earth. They reported that "on earth there is no such splendour or such beauty, and we are at a loss how to describe it. We only know that God dwells there among men, and their service is fairer than the ceremonies of other nations. For we cannot forget that beauty. Every man, after tasting something sweet, is afterward unwilling to accept that which is bitter, and therefore we cannot dwell longer here." When the prince and the boyars heard that report they accepted the Greek Christian faith and were baptized.

The Divine Liturgy is a religious drama in three acts: first is the Offertory, or *Proscomide,* in which the priest prepares the gifts which will be transformed into the body and the blood of Christ; second, the Liturgy of the Catechumens, and third, the Liturgy of the Faithful. Each one of these three stages is divided into briefer acts, all of which reach a climax in the crucifixion and the resurrection of Christ. The meaning of the Offertory prayers is the redeeming plan of God which became manifest through the prophets and reached its climax in the person of Christ. The priest recites several prayers and verses from the Psalms and the Book of Isaiah, which describe Christ as the lamb who was led to the slaughter for the redemption of the world (Isa. 53:6-8).

One of the significant parts of the First Act is the commemoration of the saints of both the Old and the New Testaments. All the elect of God are gathered together into the bosom of the Church. The Church in heaven, or Church triumphant, and the Church on earth, or Church militant, are united into a living and inseparable organism of God. The angelic powers, the Old Testament prophets and patriarchs, the Mother of Jesus, the Apostles, martyrs, Fathers, and saints of the Christian Church are invoked for their brethren on earth. The commemoration of the believers, dead or alive, constitutes another section of the Offertory.

The Second Act is rather instructive for members

79

and future members of the Church. The petitions and doxologies culminate in the reading of the Scriptures, the sermon, and several prayers for the catechumens. The Third Act, however, is the most important of the one-hour drama of the Liturgy. The great entrance, during which the gifts are transferred from the Offertory and are placed on the Holy Altar, signifies the road of our Lord to Golgotha. These are moving moments while the choir sings, "We who mystically represent the Cherubim, sing the thrice-holy Hymn to the life-giving Trinity. Therefore, let us put away all worldly care, so that we may welcome the King of all." The faithful are urged to intensify their participation in the Divine play.

As the centurion confessed the deity of Christ, likewise the faithful proclaim their faith by reciting the creed of the Nicaea and Constantinople synods of 325 and 381 at a certain moment of the Third Act. They proclaim their faith in God, the Father Almighty, in the one Lord Jesus Christ and in the Holy Spirit, in the Church of God and her holy Mysteries. While much of the Liturgy is mystical and sacramental, the recitation of the creed is the doctrinal confession of the faithful. The creed is an essential part of Greek Orthodox worship as are important other symbols and movements in the Church. The symbolic acts in general fulfill the vacuum which is created because of the lack of words and movements or because terms and expressions are inadequate in some stages and developments of the evolution of the Liturgy. The creed as a symbol and confessional narration bridges two important stages of the liturgical drama. It is therefore both a symbol properly so called and a confession of the essentials of the historic faith.

The bloodless sacrifice, the invocation, and the descent of the Holy Spirit upon the gifts of the Last Supper is an act in which one must participate if he is to understand its impact and effect. The heavens descend and the earth is elevated for a mystical union. The earthly and material are transubstantiated into Godly elements, the body and blood of Christ. Christ was crucified, thus giving Himself for the redemption of everyone; He takes the place of each condemned individual to release him and set him free from bondage and make him an adopted son of God. Christ gives Himself, and man partakes of His offer, in the form of bread and wine, already transubstantiated into the living Christ. It is through this participation, through Holy Communion, that man is lifted to heaven, or that heaven and earth, the supernatural and the natural, the spiritual and the material, are unified into a real communion and consummation. Dionysios the Areopagite writes: "How else can we imitate God if we do not repeat His divine life through the mystagogy of the Liturgy? The Lord ordained that the mystery of the Divine Liturgy should be constantly performed in order that we humans, however imperfect, should unite with a perfect God. As cells are united and make up the human body so the faithful are united as cells upon the body of God and partake of His holy life—otherwise, we become dead organisms, foreign to a healthy and living God."

In the Divine Liturgy the divine and the human, time and eternity, the now and the remote, spiritual longings and earthly desires, cries of distress and exclamations of joy, and several other contrasts and antinomies are united into an organism of harmony and real life.

The epilogue of the Divine Liturgy depicts the ascension of the Lord and proclaims the eschatological expectations of the Church. Christ will come once again to consummate the invisible and the visible, the divine and the human into an eternal cosmos of beauty, happiness, and life. Indeed, the ultimate purpose of the Divine Liturgy is to accomplish an intimate communion of man with God in Jesus Christ, to enrich man with God's Grace, to regenerate and make the human a new creation.

If one is to appreciate the Divine Liturgy from the beginning to the end, one is advised to attend the service of Easter Sunday. Easter service is both darkness and light, defeat and victory, lamentation and triumph. It is, however, darkness, defeat, and lamentation for a few minutes only. The Church is draped in black. Everything is reminiscent of death, the death of Christ. The Lord is laid in His tomb and His followers are plunged into fear and despair. At midnight, amid total darkness in the Church, while the cantors sing a lamentation describing a fruitless search for the body of Christ by Mary Magdalene and the other women, the priest comes forward with a lighted candle, singing, "O ye faithful, come forward and receive light from the light that never wanes." He proceeds singing the melodic hymn, "Christ is risen," in which the congregation joins in the joyful announcement of the triumph of Christ over death. The Church assumes a new color. Joy, hope, love, and eternity are the panegyric message of Easter Sunday and of every Sunday.

6

✤✤

OTHER
SACRAMENTS

B UT, THERE is always a danger of falling short of Grace of God. Sin as a treacherous enemy alienates man from God. The means for reconciliation of man with God is the sacrament of Repentance and Confession in which man returns like the prodigal son seeking forgiveness. The Church happily receives the penitent by accepting the confession. "If you forgive the sins of any, they are forgiven; if you retain the sins of any, they are retained" the Church was assured (John 20:23). Thus, Repentance and Confession make the fourth sacrament by which the regeneration of the human soul is achieved. It is the sacrament through which sinful man is "born again." Repentance is the crisis within man that calls him to a renewal of himself through the Grace of God and to a continuation of man's process of *theosis* which had been interrupted by sin. Indeed, man's divination and renewal are but a continuous repentance and confession of sinfulness.

The Orthodox Church accepts three more sacraments: Ordination or Holy Orders, Marriage, and Holy Unction. Ordination is practiced according to the evidence of the Holy Scriptures. The Bible indicates clearly that there is a distinction among the faithful of Christ, which in modern terms can be described as "clergy" and "laity." St. Luke tells us that Jesus had many disciples from whom He chose only twelve: "And . . . He [Jesus] went out into the hills to pray; and all night he continued in prayer to God. And when it was day, he called his disciples, and chose from them twelve, whom he named apostles" (Luke 6:12-13).

In the book of Acts, the same author states that the seven first deacons were elected by the faithful and ordained by the twelve Apostles. The seven candidates were "set before the apostles, and when they

had prayed, the apostles laid their hands upon them"
(Acts 6:6). Likewise, when Barnabas and Paul were
sent out to evangelize, the twelve, after having fasted
and prayed, "laid their hands on them" (Acts 13:3).

The above verses testify openly against those who
do not accept Holy Orders as a distinct ministry of
the Church, or those who do not differentiate clergymen from laymen. The ministry of ordination was
transmitted to disciples of the Apostles (see 1 Tim.
4:14; 2 Tim. 1:16, etc.), thus preserving the continuity and Apostolic succession of the Church to the
present day.

Deacon, presbyter, and bishop are the offices of the
Church. In the Orthodox Church a future clergyman
has a choice either of marrying or of remaining single.
There are married and unmarried deacons and presbyters. The bishops, however, are elected from the
unmarried priests. They are free from family cares so
that they may be wholeheartedly devoted to the
service of the Church. The supreme governing body
is the totality of the bishops known as the Synod,
which professes Jesus as its Head.

Through the Mystery of marriage two individuals
are united into one, and in this union they live the
same kind of life, and follow the same road—that of
virtue and holiness. By this sacrament the union of

two human bodies and spirits is blessed for the pro-
creation of mankind and the integration of their personalities. Life itself is a great mystery, and marriage,
which is the union of two bodies and two minds for
the creation of a new life, could not be anything less.

Accepting marriage as a lifelong unity, the Orthodox Church opposes the dissolution of the matrimo-
nial vows "saving for the cause of fornication" (Mark
2:27). Divorce is granted on several grounds. Once it
is granted the Church does allow a second marriage.

Intermarriage between Orthodox and non-Orthodox is never encouraged, because of the complica-
tions involved in such a marriage. In case a mixed
marriage is not averted, an understanding is made
that the children born of the union will be brought up
in the Orthodox faith. However, the non-Orthodox
member is not obliged to join the Orthodox Church.

The Church encourages child-bearing as a blessing
of God. Abortion is equated to murder: "Those who
give drugs for procuring abortion, and those who receive poisons to kill the fetus, are subjected to
the penalty of murder" (91 canon of the Quinisext
Council). But there is no unanimity of opinion on
birth control in the Orthodox Catholic Church as a
whole. The Church of Greece has come out against
birth control and the Greek Archdiocese of North and

South America has made a similar declaration. While it is not encouraged by the Greek Church in general, the Church makes exceptions in certain cases. When a mother's health is at stake "the Orthodox confessor is not expected to advise his people to disregard the scientific opinion. He is rather bound to tell the spouses concerned to follow their doctor's advice," as one authority has put it. There is no specific canon of any general Council which would bind the whole Church on the matter. The emphasis is always placed on the sacredness of marriage and our trust in God.

The sacrament of Holy Unction is intended for the health of the human body. It is a sacrament primarily for the sick and it can be rightly called a healing service. It is based on the well-known passage in the Scriptures: "Is any one among you sick? Let him call for the presbysters of the Church, and let them pray over him, anointing him with oil in the name of the Lord; and the prayer of faith will save the sick man" (James 5:14).

Healing in the Church stands or falls with our concept of Christ. If Christ were both the physician of the human soul and the healer of man's body, as the Gospels present Him, then His Church cannot be anything less. Jesus' ministry of healing is summarized by St. Matthew as follows: "And Jesus was going

88

about all the towns and villages . . . curing every kind of disease and infirmity" (Matt. 9:35). Matthew adds that Christ, having summoned His disciples, gave them power over unclean spirits, to cast them out, and to cure every kind of disease and infirmity (Matt. 10:1). This charismatic attribute of Jesus was given to His Church.

The Orthodox Church practices this ministry of healing today, using oil as the outward sign of the therapeutic Grace of God. The Church continues the Apostolic practice which is described by St. Mark as follows: Going forth in their ministry "they [the disciples] preached that men should repent, and they cast out many devils, and anointed with oil many sick people and healed them" (Mark 6:13). It is fully confirmed that the ancient Christian Church practiced this Mystery of Unction for the physical cure of the sick faithful. The remission of sins is a secondary effect of the sacrament.

Among these sacraments, Sacred Confession and Holy Unction are the least widely or frequently used.

7

TRADITIONAL PRACTICES IN ORTHODOXY

FROM WHAT SOURCES does the Orthodox Church derive her faith? The creed is based upon Divine Revelation as incorporated in the life of the Church and the Holy Scriptures. Divine Revelation became manifest to man "at sundry times and in divers manners" (Heb. 1:1) and it has been deposited in the Church as Scripture and Tradition. Its integrity and authenticity are protected by the Holy Spirit Who remains with the Church forever (John 19:26). The primitive Church did not have the Bible as we know it today. And yet the Church lived according to Divine Revelation which, with the final screening and codification of the Canon, was understood as Sacred Tradition and Holy Scriptures. One cannot overemphasize the biblical character of the Greek Orthodox Church, for, ironically, members of certain Christian denominations often accuse the Greek Orthodox Catholic Church of neglect in making use of the Bible. They usually label her as a Church involved extensively in symbolism and ritual.

Such a notion of the Orthodox is not justified. And as a matter of fact the contrary is true. The truth is that the Holy Scriptures occupy a prominent place in the life, thought, and worship of the Orthodox Church. For the Greek Orthodox Catholic Church is very much a scriptural Church. She is the biblical Church par excellence. It is not only that her faith is derived from the Holy Scriptures, but also her very life is deeply imbued with ideas, teachings, and the ethos of the Bible. The various forms of worship and the liturgical life of the Church bear the seal of the Bible to an admirable degree.

There is no sacrament, liturgy, or service in the Orthodox Church which does not include selections from the Scriptures. Both the Old and the New Testaments are used often. Since the Old Testament is the "paedagogus" leading to Christ, it is used in such services as the vespers and the *orthros*. Passages from Genesis, Exodus, Isaiah, Jonah, and other Old Testament books, especially the Psalms, are read in each vesper service as well as in the Sunday morning service before the Divine Liturgy. Each Liturgy includes two New Testament selections, one from the Acts or the Epistles and the second from one of the Gospels. These various "pericopes" from the Psalms, prophecies, Gospels, and Epistles constitute an integral part of each service in the Orthodox Church today.

But the claim of the Orthodox Catholic Church for her scriptural character is not based exclusively on the aforementioned scriptural readings. Her prayer life, hymns, and rites are imbued with, one might almost say permeated by, scriptural spirituality, verses and elements. Every prayer and hymn of each Liturgy, sacrament, or service includes scriptural material and expresses some biblical event. It is true that certain services are more scriptural than others and that the number and extent of the scriptural element vary from service to service, but whatever the ratio may be, it is certain that each service is based on some biblical truth.

There are certain books which enjoy a considerable popularity. The Psalms, Genesis, and Isaiah are more popular than any other Old Testament book. Exodus and Wisdom of Solomon follow. From the New Testament books Matthew, Luke, 1 Corinthians, Romans, the Gospel of John, and the Epistle to the Hebrews precede all others in that order.

Hymnology is similarly oriented in Scripture. Most of it has been inspired by some event narrated in the Scriptures or by some truth expressed in them.

There is much evidence that an intense reverence for the Holy Scriptures exists in the Orthodox Church. The study of the Bible has always been encouraged; in fact, even the illiterate in the Orthodox world have committed whole Psalms and other portions of the Scriptures to memory. The writings not only of the liturgical authors but of the Fathers, teachers, and doctors of the Church, in general, are impregnated with scriptural verses and expressions.

A practice in the early Church, that persons had to know parts of the Bible by heart, and that candidates for the Priesthood were impelled to learn a certain number of Psalms, plus a Gospel and several Epistles before ordination, is not required in the Church today. Nonetheless, scriptural sayings and elements are in the mouths of the faithful in Orthodox lands like proverbs and mottoes.

The Word of God is the inexhaustible source of

spiritual instruction and nurture in the Orthodox
Catholic Church today. The Orthodox faithful are
urged to study the Bible diligently and to make it
the guide of their lives.

Thus, it is emphasized that the Holy Scriptures,
which have saturated the liturgical books and the
hymnology of the Church, indeed occupy a central
place in the Orthodox life and worship today.

But the "biblical" character of the Church should
not be emphasized at the expense of its "traditional"
side. The latter is a strong characteristic and of equal
importance to the biblical character of the Church.
Sacred Tradition is not an accumulation of human
sayings which have been transmitted to us. It is rather the life of the Church under the constant guid-
ance of the Holy Spirit. God the Father created the
world; God the Son redeemed sinful man; and God
the Holy Spirit perpetuates the Redemptive work of
Christ sanctifying and leading the Church. Sacred
Tradition is the handiwork of the Holy Spirit in the
life and the thought of the Church.

The doctrines of all Christendom about the Holy
Trinity, the natures of Christ, and the function of the
Holy Spirit are some of the teachings of the Sacred Tradition. These teachings were formulated by
the universal Church when her hierachy convened

in ecumenical or local councils. Sacred Tradition is the revelation of the Holy Spirit to the Church that is incorporated in the doctrinal life of the Church. This is in perfect agreement with the promise of Christ. He said to His disciples: "When the Spirit of truth comes, he will guide you into all the truth; for he will not speak on his own authority but whatever he hears he will speak, and he will declare to you the things that are to come" (John 16:13). Because of her confidence in and attachment to the Person of the Holy Spirit, the Orthodox has remained a pneumatological Church.

And while Holy Scriptures have been established as we know them today, Sacred Tradition is the faith to which the Church Councils and the Fathers of Christianity bear witness and of which the Orthodox Church is the vigilant and abiding custodian.

Sacred icons, the cross, candles, and the like, found in an Orthodox house of worship, are not elements of Sacred Tradition, which deal with doctrine and faith but, rather, they constitute a heritage of tradition. They are only symbols intended to help in the religious instruction of the faithful. They correspond to the needs of the human senses and are in no way idolatrous. A distinction should be made between tradition and Sacred Tradition. The former is human and the latter is divine. There is much ritualism and symbolism in the worship of the Orthodox Church. Of course a great deal of it can be traced back to the Old Testament times, while a portion owes its origin to the religious tradition of antiquity. For example, incense is used in the Church because the believers ask God to accept their prayers "as incense before Him." The faithful make the sign of the cross to remind themselves that the Son of God was crucified for their salvation. The outward symbol of the cross is the expression of an inner conversation with God. These elements constitute tradition.

Icons of Jesus Christ, His Mother, the patriarchs of the Old Testament, the Apostles, the saints and the martyrs are found in Orthodox houses of worship and in most Orthodox homes. They are used to emphasize the living reality of the sacred persons depicted on them. There is in the Orthodox Church a strong feeling of the reality of the supernatural. There is no death, but life, whether upon the earth or beyond it. Thus, the celestial beings are united with the terrestrial humanity in the bosom of the *Ecclesia* which transcends both time and space. "The earth is the Lord's and the fullness thereof; the world, and all that dwells in it" (Ps. 24:1). All were made by God and belong to God. All were made for the service of man and to be used for the instruction of man. There is nothing pagan in symbolism so long as it remains a means and not an end in itself. There is nothing idolatrous which is pious, ethical, and morally instructive. On this basis is the use of symbolism in the life of the individual and the life of the Church understood.

Abuses can and do happen in every sphere of life, whether we are aware of them or not. It is possible for the individual Christian to make an icon the object not of respect, but of worship. Similarly, it is equally possible for someone to abuse the meaning and the significance of the Holy Scriptures and become a bibliolater.

Man lives by symbols and rituals, whether he realizes it or not. Therefore, as long as they lead one to virtue and piety there is nothing alarming about them. As long as they remain means and people do not repose their trust in them, they can have a place in the religious life of the faithful. Icons and symbols express much that words cannot convey.

The dictates of nature which urge man to be good and spiritually wholesome may be followed provided that man is endowed with faith and knowledge of his Christian creed. What agrees with man's mind and heart agrees with God's teaching. These elements of

Orthodox worship do not necessarily obscure the simplicity of the Christian truth. That more simplicity is required today of the Orthodox Church no Orthodox Christian denies. Nevertheless, the use of ritual and symbolism to a limited measure is not only permissible but desirable to the human heart and mind. They are elements of disposition rather than of cold logic, a natural part of life rather than an academic disputation, a source of inspiration and instruction rather than of knowledge and learning.

In brief, ritualism and symbolism in the Orthodox Church constitute an object lesson and a graphic representation of the persons or things of the celestial *Ecclesia* and not actualities in themselves.

It is important to note here that though the Church allows the depiction of Christ in His human form, she never permits the separation of the divine from the human element. Thus an icon of Christ is always an icon of the God-man Christ. And icons of the Theotocos, the saints, the angels, and the other figures of the supernatural Church are not realistic representations but depictions and projections of the virtues and the saintliness of the personalities involved. Heavenly personalities are presented to mortals who are expected to imitate them and achieve perfection in God.

Thus, Divine Revelation deposited in and guarded by the Church is the source of the Greek Orthodox Catholic faith—one fountain but two channels, i.e., Sacred Tradition and the Holy Scriptures.

In short, the Orthodox Church appeals to Divine Revelation as incorporated in the Holy Scriptures and the Sacred Tradition, to the ancient Fathers and the ecumenical and local councils, and realizes an unbroken continuity with the original Church, not only in her faith, sacramental or prayer life, but also in her culture and administration.

Again, this emphasizes the fact that the Orthodox Church today is in full agreement with the ancient Church in all essentials of doctrine and order.

If the Orthodox Church makes such claims, must she not be intolerant and isolated? The contrary is true. Although the Church believes and claims that she is the true Church, there is tolerance, understanding, cooperation, and love toward others. In fact, this Church willingly listens to views of others. There is freedom in the Church but discipline and authority as well.

The Orthodox Church, despite her convictions and adamant position in matters of faith, is anxious to participate in such organizations as the National Council of Churches in the United States and in the

The Greek Orthodox Church

World Council of Churches. While very few, if any,
Protestant or Roman Catholic clergymen or theologians study in Greek Orthodox theological schools,
many of the Orthodox clergy and theologians do
study in Protestant or Roman Catholic theological institutions without jeopardy. The Orthodox Church
works and prays for the integration of all Christians in
faith, in love, and in hope within the true Church,
which is Christ on earth perpetuated into the ages
until His second coming and the last judgment. She
prays constantly "for the peace of the whole world,
for the stability of the Holy Churches of God, and for
the union of all."

Indeed, as Dr. James I. McCord, president of
Princeton Theological Seminary, writes: "The Greek
Orthodox Church is one of the pioneering bodies and
the call to unity of the Ecumenical Patriarch is one of
the milestones in ecumenical history."

She has entered into the ecumenical movement
and participates in dialogues in order to bear witness
to the ancient unadulterated faith in a confident but
fraternal manner. She is confident and unshaken because she has remained faithful to the historical, theological, cultural, and ethical ideals of early Christianity.

The Orthodox Church is the most democratic system of believers. Her clergy are elected with the ap-

proval of the laity, with very rare exceptions. Laymen play an important role in the administration of the Church. They are elected to the Executive Council of the Church, and they have great administrative responsibilities in the local parish. And all believe, all live, all worship, all belong to the same body. All may occupy a significant position, and work accordingly for the well-being of the body of the Church. All are animated by the same principles of spiritual life, the same faith, the same ethics, the same means of sanctification and communion with the Creator and Redeemer, God.

The Orthodox Church does not believe in authoritarian systems. She preserves the ancient system of administration known as synodic, which is neither absolutist nor so loose as to encourage anarchy and extreme individualism. An examination of her administration will illustrate her system of freedom and discipline. A deacon serves a presbyter in a parish or a bishop in his diocese. A presbyter or a priest is the center of spiritual authority over his parish, receiving his authority from the bishop. And the bishop is the head of the Church in a given district or diocese. But over the local bishop stands the Synod or the totality of the bishops. Jesus Christ is the head of the Synod and the Church as a whole.

8

✦✦✦✦✦✦✦✦✦✦✦✦✦✦✦✦✦✦✦✦✦✦✦✦✦✦✦✦✦✦✦✦✦✦✦✦✦✦

A CHURCH
OF SAINTS AND
HOLY FATHERS

THE GREEK ORTHODOX CHURCH is also a patristic Church, that is, a church which honors many Fathers and saints. This is one of the distinct characteristics of Greek Orthodoxy, and one cannot fail to observe that Orthodox Christians speak with reverence for and devotion to the numerous saints and Fathers of the Church. The memory of one saint or as many as two thousand saints is observed in one single day, and several Sundays of the ecclesiastical year are put aside for a certain group of Church Fathers, such as the Fathers of the First Ecumenical Council, those of the Second, or of the Seventh.

Patriarchs and personalities of the Old Testament era as well as saints and Fathers of the New Testament times and the long history of Christianity are invoked in every service of the Orthodox Church. The *Ecclesia* includes all the people of God who lived either before or after the incarnation of the eternal *Logos,* and the people of the Old Testament are honored just as much as the saints of the New Covenant. This concept is well expressed in the following prayer from the service of *orthros:*

"O God, save thy people, and bless thine inheritance; visit thy world with mercies and bounties. Exalt the estate of orthodox Christians, and bestow upon us thy rich blessings. We ask all these through the intercessions of our all-holy Theotocos and ever-virgin Mary; by the might of the precious and life-giving Cross; by the protection of the honorable heavenly angelic powers; at the supplications of the honorable, glorious prophet, fore-runner and baptist John; of the holy, glorious and all-laudable Apostles; of all the Fathers among the saints, the great hierarchs and ecumenical teachers . . . of the holy, glorious and right-victorious martyrs; of our venerable and God-bearing Fathers; of the holy and righteous ancestors of God [Jesus] Joachim and Anna; of Saint or Saints . . . , whose memory we celebrate, and of all thy saints, we beseech thee . . . have mercy upon us."

During the Offertory service, or *prothesis*, the priest commemorates many Old Testament prophets, such as Moses, Aaron, Elijah, Elisha, David, Daniel, and others. The world before Christ and the world after Him who made up the chosen people are commemorated and united into the bosom of the Church, whose head is Christ Himself. Thus the angels, the prophets, and the holy men of ancient Israel, the Mother of Christ, the Apostles, the unknown martyrs, the great Fathers, and the humble holy men of the desert are united and honored by the faithful.

But why is so much emphasis laid on the saints? Why is there so much prominence paid to the Church Fathers? The answer is closely related to the conception of the Orthodox about the nature of the Church. The saints and the Fathers constitute the conscience of the *Ecclesia* because they were the living flame of the Holy Spirit. They were people who experienced the presence of Christ in their lives and became witnesses of this fact to the world. As a result of this devotion some of them even gave their lives for Christ. The blood they shed for the faith, the oral and the written word they proclaimed, the hymns and the services they wrote compose the life of the Church. Thus they have made themselves eternally present in the earthly Church.

The Orthodox believe that the saints and the holy men are always present in the faith and life of their Church. They are the perpetual teachers of the gospel and the supreme personification of the life of Christ. The Fathers became the sure and most authentic guides in the understanding and in the propagation of the faith. They comprise the pattern of a genuine devotion to the spirit of early Christianity and remain as living examples of the spirit of Pentecost. As heralds of the Holy Spirit the Fathers purified the faith from heretical influences and defined all the major doctrines of Christianity, such as the Holy Trinity, the natures of Christ, the Person of the Holy Spirit, the nature of the Church, and the function of her sacraments. They became "the golden mouths of the Logos . . . the sweet-smelling flowers of Paradise, illuminating stars of the world and the glory of mankind," as we sing in one of the many hymns.

The Fathers, together with the martyrs and the ascetics, supported the Church and strengthened the faith. The blood of the martyrs nourished the seeds of this early devotion, and from this sacrifice arose the great tree of Christendom.

Numerous are the saints, martyrs, and Fathers

honored in the Greek Orthodox Church. From St. Stephen, the first martyr, down to St. Chrysostomos, Bishop of Smyrna in the 1920's, we may mention the most popular, such as St. Polycarpos, St. Ignatios, St. Anthony, St. Athanasios, St. Basil the Great, St. Gregory of Nazianzos, St. John Chrysostomos, St. George, St. Demetrios, St. Theodore, St. Eustathios, St. Maximos the Confessor, St. John of Damascus, St. Photios, St. Philaretos the Alms-Giver, St. John Vatatzes, St. Gregory Palamas, St. George the New Martyr, St. Nicodemos the Hagiorite, and St. Nektarios of Salamis. Some of them were simple folk, others were theologians and clergymen, still others were wise men and scholars, while there were even kings and socially prominent people who considered "the sufferings of this present time not worthy compared with the glory that is to be revealed . . ." (Rom. 8:18).

The Greek Orthodox Church not only honors the saints but also projects them, urging the faithful to imitate their faith and life.

But does the Orthodox Church have anything unique to offer to the world today? Is she relevant to our time? What is her message to modern man?

9

****

A CHURCH
OF OPTIMISM
AND HOPE

W<small>E</small> <small>BELIEVE</small> that Orthodoxy can illuminate modern man with a light all her own. Orthodoxy is, indeed, very relevant to our times. It is not only that this *Ecclesia*, both in its religious meaning and in its secular connotation, has preserved faithfully the *orthodoxia*, the catholicity, and the consciousness of the original Christian faith; the Orthodox Church has preserved the ethos, the very essence of the teaching of Christ, i.e., the ethics of agape, of *philanthropia*.

Orthodoxy stands on the optimistic side of the conflicting ideologies and creeds of the twentieth century. Western Christendom suffers from a number of dilemmas, such as the opposition of nature to grace, faith to works, the oral word to the sacrament, Scripture to Tradition, the clergy to the laity, and other theological problems. The Orthodox Church has no such dilemmas and confusions. She is a Church which emphasizes a natural revelation in harmony with revealed grace, faith and good works, the word and the sacrament, Bible and Tradition, clergy and laity. In contrast to the pessimism and false anxiety of Latin or Nordic Christianity, Orthodoxy is optimistic because of its belief in the dignity of man; because of its doctrine of the deification of human nature under God; because of its belief in the philanthropia of God for man, and in the philanthropia of man for man. The gospel of the Orthodox *Ecclesia* is the gospel of the resurrection, of triumph, and of victory. For in Orthodoxy man does not stand alone. Greek Orthodoxy believes that there is no history but only holy history; that God reigns supreme and all evolve under His watchful providence and plans.

The whole system of Orthodox thought and teaching is based on God as the Supreme Being of life and existence, and on man as the image and the likeness of God and the masterpiece of God's creative power.

The significance that Orthodoxy places on man can be considered its unique contribution to modern thought. What is man? Is he a sum of chemical compounds, i.e., some water, some phosphorous, some fat, etc.? Is he simply a social being, a being which cannot live alone? Or is man an insatiable sexual being?

To the Orthodox Church, man is much more than a biological being, a social animal, or simply a sexual phenomenon. Man is a dependent being. He was not self-made; God made man. Man is a psychosomatic entity, a being made of dust and deity. He was made "but a little less than God" (Ps. 8:5) and at the same time "he is like the beasts that perish" (Ps. 49:12). He is a sinner, a rebel against his Creator. Nevertheless, this defection is not a total one. Man can be restored through God and man's half-brother Jesus Christ. Christ personifies the Grace and philanthropia of God, as St. Paul assures us (Tit. 3:4). Philanthropia, then, is the governing element between God and man, God's love for man. In an analogous way the Church teaches that the power which should regulate the lives of men is again the attribute of philanthropia—agape. This element of philanthropia is a unique contribution that the Orthodox Church can make to the modern world. On this basis alone Orthodoxy is very relevant to our times. Philanthropia is the answer to the agony and spiritual isolation of modern man—philanthropia of God for man, and philanthropia of man for man. This notion is both Greek and Christian.

The Orthodox Church emphasizes brotherly love not only for her members and toward other Christian believers, but philanthropia for all humanity. It is a fundamental doctrine of the Orthodox faith that all men are created equal and after the image of God; for God there is no colored and white, male and female, Greek, American, Jew, Puerto Rican, or Anglo-Saxon. Christ restored this human image which had been almost destroyed because of man's rebellion against God. The death of Christ was the supreme expression of the philanthropia of God for man. And because of the philanthropia of God, all men are called to a resurrection, to the new restoration that was accomplished by the resurrection of Christ.

Man is not simply an animal struggling and constantly fighting for survival, or a product of some evolutionary process. Man's spirit, his ability to think, and the unfulfilled vacuum within himself and his creative abilities indicate clearly that man is unique, different, and superior to the rest of the living creatures. Man is called to *theosis,* as the Fathers of the Church have put it; that is, man is called to deification. It was when man forgot his destiny that the love and the philanthropia of God took the initiative to restore man to his previous state of divine origin.

It is relevant, of course, to remind ourselves that the notion of the ancient Greeks about man has much in common with the Christian view. For the Pythagorean philosophers the spirit of man is simply a fallen deity imprisoned in the human body. And for the Stoic philosophers the soul of man is a spark of divinity which upon death returns to the universal God. But while in Greek antiquity the divine element within us is assimilated by the universal deity upon death, within Christanity man preserves his individuality. And this is attributed again to the Grace and the philanthropia or agape of God for man. Man is not only the supreme being upon the earth, but an immortal being as well.

Here then must we seek the basis for optimism about man. God loves man, and in return God seeks man's love for man. Here lies the unique contribution of Orthodoxy.

The concept of philanthropia stems from the teaching of the brotherhood of man. And our brotherhood is best expressed through the life and activity of the terrestrial *Ecclesia*. When the Orthodox participate in the Holy Eucharist, they are united not only with the risen Christ, but among themselves as well. What Orthodoxy is preaching is love, for "if anyone says 'I love God' and hates his brother, he is a liar; for he who does not love his brother whom he has seen, cannot love God whom he has not seen" (1 John 4:20).

Orthodoxy's gospel of philanthropia is beautifully expressed in a hymn of the resurrection, which proclaims: "Let us embrace one another. Let those who hate us speak to us: 'Brethren, for the sake of the Resurrection we will all forgive one another'; and so let us cry out: Christ rose from the dead after destroying death by death; he gives life to all . . . ."

So it is an act of love when men forgive one another; it is an act of love when men pray for each other. It is an act of love when they humble themselves before each other. Thus, in an age of anxiety and degradation of human nature, Christianity's gospel of God's love for man must find an analogous response of man's love for man. Indeed we "owe no one anything, except to love one another" (Rom. 13:8) as "God so loved the world that he gave his only begotten son, that whoever believes in him should not perish but have eternal life" (John 3:16).

The Orthodox Church pleads with the enemies of humanity; she begs of the dictators and the individuals who are thirsty for power and vanity to love and spare man. The Orthodox Church, which has tasted the brutalities of man, pleads for sanity and understanding among the powerful of the earth lest they recklessly destroy man, the image and masterpiece of God. Orthodoxy pleads that we not destroy man, that we not degrade man; instead that each of us help him, whosoever he may be, whatever he may believe, assist him materially and spiritually to reach a maturity and a happy life upon the earth and to reach his godliness, his sainthood and his *theosis* by the grace and the help of God through Jesus Christ.

Much ecumenical discussion is being conducted by Christian Churches of all creeds. Theologians and ecclesiastics are seeking formulas by which the Christian Churches would join hands and achieve unity. Orthodoxy's message to the Christian world can be summed up in the words of St. Peter: "Let us love one another earnestly from the heart . . . having purified our souls by our obedience to the truth . . . through the living and abiding word of God" (1 Pet. 1:22-23).

10

✤✤✤✤✤✤✤✤✤✤✤✤✤✤✤✤✤✤✤✤✤✤✤✤✤✤✤✤✤✤✤✤✤✤✤

THE CHURCH
IN AMERICA

T HE ORTHODOX CATHOLIC CHURCH IN AMERICA,
whether known as Greek or Hellenic, Russian or
Ukrainian, Syrian or Serbian, etc., is the same
Church, preserving the same principles, culture, and
administration as those of the undivided Christian
Church. She proclaims the gospel of Christ not only
through teaching and preaching but also by such
means as charitable institutions, orphanages, old-age
homes, and institutions of higher learning.

In the United States there are several Orthodox orphanages and old-age homes. There are six theological schools for the ministerial needs of the Churches. In addition there are several periodicals. Considering the circumstances under which the Orthodox Church was established in America, the short time of her residence here, the financial, social, and educational barriers that she had to overcome these last fifty years, we may conclude that the Old Church has made consistent and appreciable progress in the New World. But despite the fact that Orthodoxy is a constructive religious and social power in America, when religion is invited to participate in Federal, State, or even city projects, we usually hear only the names of the Protestant, Roman Catholic, and Jewish faiths as participants. Only those are mentioned as the major religious faiths in America.

But if we investigate the religious make-up of the American people and if we attempt to examine the churches and houses of worship of any medium- or large-sized city, it will be discovered that there is a fourth major religion among us. There are people, churches, and institutions which express a religious tradition dissimilar to any of the aforementioned faiths. Antiquity and modernity, the historic past and the living present are blended together to give us the picture of the Greek or Eastern Orthodox Christian faith.

A considerable portion of the American people profess the Christian Greek Orthodox faith. Admittedly, this is a new religious faith in America, approximately fifty years of age. Nevertheless, it is as old as Christianity itself. It ranks fifth among the great religions of the world and second among the Christian Churches.

The *Yearbook of American Churches,* published by the National Council of the Churches of Christ in the U.S.A., reports that there are just over three million Orthodox Christians in the United States. But this must be viewed as a very conservative number since many Eastern Orthodox Churches consider family units rather than individuals as members. There are, more accurately, over five million Greek Orthodox Christians in America. The American Orthodox Churches belong to jurisdictions which bear national names, but they all profess the same faith and are bound closely by the same principles of doctrine, worship, and ethics.

These churches are only administratively separate. Intercommunion among them makes them essentially one Church. Thus, though one may hear vari-

ous names, e.g., Hellenic Orthodox, Russian Orthodox, Serbian Orthodox, Ukrainian Orthodox, Syrian
Orthodox, etc., he must identify all with the same
one historic faith, the Greek or Eastern Orthodox.
Why, then, is it not recognized as a major faith
in America?

The fact that the majority of the American people
do not know much about the Greek Orthodox must be
partially attributed to various Federal, State, and
city agencies; to the press and communications; and
to universities and institutions which have ignored
Orthodoxy for many years. Today it is impera-
tive that this religion receive its full partnership in
the religious life of the nation.

From the cultural point of view, Greek Orthodoxy
should not be foreign to the Americans who have had
some elementary education. Our present American
culture is a reflection of this Greek-Christian tradition. And Greek or Eastern Orthodoxy is nothing less.
It is a harmonious concurrence between Greek ideals
and Christian faith, and both are very much alive
today in America.

Greek ideals are present and move in any direction
we turn. The concepts of democracy, moderation,
beauty, truth, and good have come down to us from
the ancient Greeks. Love, the supreme virtue and

fulfillment of all religions, is certainly a Christian contribution.

Thus Greek Orthodoxy is not a remote and mysterious religion. It is erroneous to identify Orthodoxy with either the Roman or the Protestant churches as various agencies and institutions sometimes do. Historically speaking, she is the original Church of Christ teaching about God, Jesus Christ, the Holy Spirit, the very *kerygma*, the *ipsissima verba* of the undivided Church as we have pointed out elsewhere.

After reading an article about Orthodoxy, a young college graduate wrote recently, "Now I understand that the Greek Orthodoxy is not a division of the Roman Church but the ancient, unadulterated Christian faith." As a unique Church she cannot be subordinated under any other. This fact is being realized more and more in our time. In fact, in recent years the focus is turned increasingly upon it not only in Western European countries, but in America as well. National magazines such as *Look, Life, Newsweek* and such non-Orthodox journals as *Jubilee, Christian Herald, Christian Century, The Living Church,* and others frequently report about Greek Orthodoxy in America. In two recent presidential inaugurations, those of President Eisenhower and President Kennedy, Greek Orthodoxy was invited to participate and pray for the new Presidents. A Senate bill was instrumental in the designation of the Eastern Orthodox faith as a separate religion in the armed forces. More than half of the states have passed legislation recognizing Greek or Eastern Orthodoxy as a major religious faith, and Orthodox chaplains now serve in veterans' hospitals, reformatory institutions, and universities.

But all these manifestations, though encouraging and hopeful, are not sufficient.

Greek Orthodoxy deserves to be designated officially as a major faith. When religion is called upon by any Federal, State, and city agency to participate in projects, discussions, or prayers, Orthodoxy should be invited. Federal action is needed to ensure that no discrimination is practiced by any organization and agency. A few years ago Senators Clifford P. Case, Everett Dirksen, and Leverett Saltonstall supported such a move, and Senator Case introduced a bill to that effect.

Nevertheless when we propose that Federal action is needed, we are aware that there are no laws which recognize any other faith, Protestant, Roman Catholic, or Jewish, as a major faith. But this is true only *de jure,* for *de facto* they are acknowledged as major faiths, an acknowledgment which is as legal as if legislation had been acted upon. The Orthodox Church has been contributing all its resources to our American society for more than fifty years. It is a Church which has made many sacrifices for the peace of the world and the propagation of democracy. More than 30,000 Orthodox Christians were killed by the Communists during the 1920's in Russia. And God only knows how many have become martyrs behind the Iron Curtain in recent years because of their religious convictions. We have heard much in America about dignitaries of other religious faiths who were persecuted by the Communists but we are little informed about the thousands of Orthodox Christians who were executed by them. We have heard nothing about the execution of more than 400 clergymen of Greece who were martyred under the torment of the Nazis and the Communists.

The Greek Orthodox Church has been a bulwark against totalitarian regimes and a champion of freedom. She has produced here in America loyal citizens and she exerts a great constructive influence upon her faithful today.

There are numerous United States citizens of the Greek Orthodox Church who occupy distinguished positions in American life. They are in the domain of science, in the fields of politics and statesmanship, of business, of music, of sports, and of other areas of activity. Many university professors, scientists, professional and business people who are devoted Greek Orthodox Christians serve the various needs of our country.

To speak in particular of the Greek branch of the Orthodox Church in America, we may point out that it is acknowledged that though the Church is a newcomer to the American continent, she has contributed greatly to the religious and cultural milieu of the American scene. For example, the *New York Times* in a recent editiorial spoke of the "two million Americans of Greek descent" as "influential and articulate" in matters affecting Greece and the affairs of the community in the New World. This important recognition demonstrates that the Greek-American community today constitutes a significant entity.

It is an indisputable fact that in the last twenty years the Greek-Americans have made significant strides, both as individuals and as a group. Most are members of middle-income families, and many, especially among the second generation, boast considerable achievements in science, in belles-lettres and the arts, and in the political and social spheres of American life, despite the fact that most Greek immigrants had little or no formal education.

The Greek Orthodox Church

It should suffice to mention in passing that more than 250 Greek-Americans are holding the rank of assistant professor or higher at American universities and that elementary and high school teachers are estimated to number five to six thousand. There is no Greek-American community that does not boast of its Greek doctors, lawyers, pharmacists, chemists, engineers, and other scientists. These are in addition to the many internationally famous scholars and scientists. For example: the historians Peter Charanis of Rutgers University, Milton Anastos and Theodore Saloutos of the University of California, George Arnakis of the University of Texas, and L. S. Stavrianos of Northwestern University; the surgeon and professor of medicine Panagiotes Constantinople of Georgetown University; the philosophers Raphael Demos of Harvard University and Gregory Vlastos of Princeton; the classicists James Notopoulos of Trinity College and Demetrios Georgacas of the University of North Dakota; the archaeologist George Mylonas of Washington University; the leading areonautical engineer Costas Pappas; the nuclear physicists Elias Gyftopoulos and George Hatzopoulos, both of the Massachusetts Institute of Technology; the mycologist Constantine Alexopoulos of the University of Texas. These are but a few of the many whose names

122

appear in *Who's Who in America, Who's Who in Higher Education,* and *Who's Who in Science.*

The church organization and the religious education of the Greek-Americans are also of considerable interest. According to recent statistics of the Greek Archdiocese of North and South America, the Orthodox Church has 424 churches served by 525 clergymen; 609 Sunday schools with 62,574 students; fourteen fully accredited schools with 3,016 students; 515 "afternoon" community schools that teach Greek to 18,380 students. There are 333 lay teachers, while some schools are staffed by parish priests. A recently undertaken effort to establish community nursery and kindergarten schools already has produced some 48 schools serving 682 preschoolers.

Without a doubt, the Greek-American community is a useful and creative, albeit highly individualistic and distinctive, part of the American milieu; but it is also mindful of its Greek heritage.

All these are factors which indicate that the Greek Orthodox religion deserves recognition as a major faith in the United States. We are not implying that the Federal government, or any other agency, should bestow any special favors upon Orthodoxy. We concur with the explanation of Senator Case of New Jersey that such a Federal action would be "as public recognition of the fact that the American citizens of the Eastern Orthodox faith constitute a substantial segment of our community, separate from the three major faiths already designated. . . ." Federal action toward complete acceptance of Orthodoxy would reinforce the movement of the various states which have already designated Orthodoxy as a major faith. History, culture, religious freedom, and equality and justice demand that Orthodoxy be granted equal status with other religions.

SELECTED
BIBLIOGRAPHY

The following bibliography is not intended as a complete guide to the study of the history, doctrine, worship, and ethics of the Greek Orthodox Church. It contains only the works which the author considers important.

Alivizatos, Hamilcar S. *The Greek Orthodox Church* (in Greek). Athens, 1955.

Androutsos, Christos. *Dogmatics of the Orthodox Eastern Church* (in Greek). 2nd edition. Athens, 1956.

Benz, Ernst. *The Eastern Orthodox Church.* New York, 1963.

Bratsiotis, Panagiotis (ed.). *Die Orthodoxe Kirche in griechischer Sicht,* Vol. 1, Stuttgart, 1959. Vol. 2, Stuttgart, 1960.

———. *Fundamental Principles and Characteristics of the Orthodox Church* (in Greek). Athens, 1937.

The Greek Orthodox Church

Bulgakov, Sergius. *The Orthodox Church,* trans. Elizabeth S. Gram. London, 1935.

Callinicos, Constantine. *The Christian Temple and Its Rites* (in Greek). 2nd edition. Athens, 1958.

———. *The Foundations of the Faith* (in Greek). 2nd edition. Athens, 1958.

Christian Union of Scientists (eds.). *Three Essays about Orthodoxy* (in Greek). Athens, 1962.

Constantelos, Demetrios J. *Byzantine Philanthropy and Social Welfare,* Rutgers Byzantine Series, No. 4. New Brunswick, N.J., 1966.

———. "The Holy Scriptures in Greek Orthodox Worship," *The Greek Orthodox Theological Review,* Vol. XII, No. 1 (1967).

Evdokimov, P. *L'Orthodoxie.* Paris, 1959.

French, R. M. *The Eastern Orthodox Church.* London, 1951.

Gavin, Frank. *Some Aspects of Contemporary Greek Orthodox Thought.* Milwaukee, 1936.

Karmires, Ioannis. *A Synopsis of the Doctrinal Teachings of the Orthodox Catholic Church* (in Greek). Athens, 1957.

Kokkinakis, Athenagoras. *Parents and Priests as Servants of Redemption.* New York, 1958.

Lossky, Vladimir. *The Mystical Theology of the Eastern Church,* trans. from the French. London, 1957.

Meyendorff, Jean. *The Orthodox Church.* New York, 1962.

———, Afanassieff, N., Schmemann, A., Koulomzine, N.

The Primacy of Peter in the Orthodox Church. London, 1963.

A Monk of the Eastern Church, *Orthodox Spirituality.* London, 1957.

Papadopoulos, Chrysostom. *The Church of Greece* (in Greek). 2nd edition. Athens, 1954.

————. *The Orthodox Eastern Church* (in Greek). Athens, 1954.

Ploumides, B. *Introduction to Christianity* (in Greek). Athens, 1959.

Schmemann, Alexander. *For the Life of the World.* New York, 1963.

————. *The Historical Road of Eastern Orthodoxy.* New York, 1963.

Theodorou, Andreas. *The Essence of Orthodoxy* (in Greek). Athens, 1961.

Theodorou, Evangelos D. *The Church of Greece.* Athens, 1959.

Trembelas, Panayotis N. *Dogmatics of the Orthodox Catholic Church,* Vol. I (in Greek). Athens, 1959.

Ware, Timothy. *The Orthodox Church.* Baltimore, 1963.

Zankov, Stefan. *The Eastern Orthodox Church,* trans. and ed. D. A. Lowrie. Milwaukee, 1929.

Zernov, Nicolas. *Eastern Christendom.* New York, 1961.

ZOE (brotherhood of theologians). *Theology—Truth and Life* (in Greek). Athens, 1962.